Show Me The Money!
Solving the mystery of ROI to unlock profits and increase company value

… a simple approach to measure and quantify the human side of business enterprise

JoAnn R. Corley
Founder, CEO | The Human Sphere™

Executive Briefing Series - #2

Show Me The Money! – *Solving the Mystery of ROI to Unlock Profits & Increase Company Value*
Written by: JoAnn R. Corley

To order this book visit www.thehumansphere.com

Library of Congress Cataloging –in- Publications available upon request.

ISBN-13: 978-1540360281

ISBN-10: 1540360288

▶ Briefing Outline ◀

"In business, the idea of measuring what you're doing,
picking the measurements that count
like customer satisfaction and performance… you thrive on that."
– Bill Gates

Preface

I've had an extraordinary professional life these past 18 plus years traveling through-out North America speaking, providing coaching and consulting services to a variety of companies. This experience has given me a ground floor and c-suite view of a variety of attitudes, philosophies and practices surrounding human resources and talent management and ultimately how a business is operated through people.

This length of time has afforded me the opportunity to witness trends (e.g. e-learning was going to replace classroom learning --- not!) as well as an evolution of how, what was once called the "personnel" department, is seen and managed.

In that time, there has been a significant evolution in the workplace: what it looks like, what people wear, the diversity of employees, titles and the role of technology, to name a few. These developments are common in most workplaces.

One area in particular that has not had a substantial evolution is in the area of human resource management. For those who disagree, hang with me. When I say human resource management, it is meant in the most literal sense. I mean how employees are seen and treated.

And while for many companies, environmental elements of the workplace have evolved, the evolution of how employees are seen and treated reflects quite a range.

Consider the following:

On one end, you have Google who is hyper-focused on and committed to the employee experience from providing transportation, to all sorts of onsite benefits. In the article Cracking Into Google: *15 Reasons Why More Than 2 Million People Apply Each Year, Google's Chief People Officer puts it this way under reason #3:*

*"3. **Caring**. No stone is left unturned in their quest to provide a welcoming work environment for employees. Actions speak louder*

than mere words. Why is caring so important to the company? According to Google's Chief People Officer Laszlo Bock:

'It turns out that the reason we're doing these things for employees is not because it's important to the business, but simply because it's the right thing to do. When it comes down to it, it's better to work for a company who cares about you than a company who doesn't. And from a company standpoint, that makes it better to care than not to care.'"

Source link:
http://www.forbes.com/sites/stanphelps/2014/08/05/cracking-into-google-the-15-reasons-why-over-2-million-people-apply-each-year/#45c35cb26c63

On the other end you have Express Scripts. They made the list of the 10 Worst Companies to Work for in the US more than once.

"Express Scripts is a third-party administrator of prescription drugs for various commercial and government health plans, and is the largest pharmacy benefit management company in the country. The average employee rating of Express Scripts is 2.5 stars out of five, tied for the lowest rating of any U.S. company. Employees commonly cite incompetent management, difficulty maintaining work-life balance, and long hours as major drawbacks for working at the company. Many employees report working 10-hour days."

You can see the complete list of 10 using this source link: http://www.huffingtonpost.com/entry/worst-companies-to-work-for_us_575b26b0e4b0e39a28ada793?ir=Business

Both examples and the explanations for the companies that made either list, relate to how employees are treated or at least *their perception* of how they are treated reflected in their ratings. And that is an important point, their perception is their reality and it's essential, in effective people management, that leaders' and managers' perceptions are aligned with those they lead.

The workplace evolution gap can really be summarized, from my observation, in this way: Companies have either moved to an employee-centered (some call it human-centric) operational and leadership approach or they are still operating from an antiquated command and control operational, leadership model and other dated employee management practices.

There's plenty of documentation to suggest human-centric leadership and operational approach is here to stay and proving to be successful. Hopefully, companies that are not evolving will soon wake up and recognize that the workforce has changed, but they have not! If not, they will continue to suffer the consequences. They sure are making it hard on themselves!

How Money is Spent is a Reflection of Values
As companies have moved into the employee, human-centric era, where company culture, employee experience, and relationship to leaders are key components, one operational consideration that many

leaders grapple with is how to wisely spend money. Some are in a perpetual quandary about how much and on what.

And, by the way, some of these leaders are baby-boomers who've had a completely different work culture experience growing up and for those who've lead, a different sensibility about money regarding how and when it should be spent. This new human centric era can challenge the values and beliefs these leaders hold dear and have contributed to their success.

However, what Marshall Goldsmith, one of the top global CEO coaches says really rings true, "What got you here, won't get you there," (a title of one of his books). To lead these kinds of companies, the philosophy

 and values of their leaders must match the need. And that's crucial, because it's from beliefs, philosophies and values that decisions are made – particularly decisions regarding money.

So in essence, how money is spent is a reflection of how a leader thinks and what is valued and their understanding of how to maximize the use of money to successfully manage and grow a company. For example, do they see spending money on and for employees as a cost or an investment? There is lots of legitimate confusion here and that is the purpose of this briefing.

You'll find this briefing particularly useful if you've ever said to yourself,

- ? "I know my leaders and managers need help, it's just not in our budget right now."
- ? "I've heard that coaching is helpful, but how can we really measure return on investment?"
- ? "We can't afford training."
- ? "Honestly, I think employee training is a waste of time and money."
- ? "How do we determine the financial impact of our employee rewards program?"

What have you or your leadership team thought or said similar to these? They and many others are extremely common and appropriately so. The ways in which money is spent for employees, particularly in the area of employee training and development, has been difficult to measure, and for many, has not gotten the results and needed returns. Though the human resource/talent management industry is still attempting to address this, for now, there is still a gapping need to put these kinds of activities into a meaningful financial context.

The need to quantify and give tangible value to this spending, if not met, will continue to stifle the growth of some companies and substantially cripple it for others. Money will not be spent to improve profitability through strategic talent management if this lack of understanding is not addressed.

What This Executive Briefing Offers
I've written this as a simple resource to meet this challenge and if applied, will enhance your company operations by way of...

✓ A brief introduction to an employee-human centric approach to leadership
✓ An introduction to the intricate role of human behavior (or what I term "people power") to operational success and how to leverage it
✓ How to read and measure human behavior
✓ How to determine and calculate the ever elusive ROI in a variety of human resource/ talent management and development initiatives.

Here's a newsflash -- there really is no mystery to ROI (sorry to be so anti-climatic so soon). It just feels or seems that way because most decision-makers don't have an practical, uncomplicated approach to determine it. That will be remedied here.

It is my firm belief that use of any of the information from this briefing will help you grow profits and company value – at least that's what my clients have experienced!

 ## Recommended Uses

✓ If you find this briefing useful and want to order additional copies for your leadership team, volume discounts are available, as well as facilitated on-site leadership roundtable to discuss insights, findings and potential applications -- great for strategic planning or a retreat.

✓ You may notice that this briefing does not strictly follow a traditional book writing format. It is designed to be a guide, a briefing for you to take notes, makes plans and to expand your knowledge around the topics discussed. For example, you won't see traditional footnoting. You'll find source links/references directly in the text for easy reference.

✓ Additionally, if you buy a physical copy, you're eligible to receive a digital version at no cost. That way you'll be able to click links, bookmark etc., right online. Just send some proof of purchase (picture of the book or receipt) to joann@thehumansphere.com.

Here to support your continued growth & success!

JoAnn

*"Leaders think and talk about the solutions.
Followers think and talk about the problems."*
-Brian Tracy

INTRODUCTION

As of this writing...

there is a great television show airing called The Profit. It's an entertaining look at how Marcus Lemonis seeks to rescue capsized companies to right size and grow them. As Marcus attempts to do so, you get an intimate view of the personalities, personal issues, relational dynamics, level of skills and capabilities (among other factors) of key players and company owners that have contributed to their current state.

Though the overall point of the program is to helping failing companies and champion the American Dream, it's also a highly instructive course in human behavior and its undeniable, unavoidable role in business success – or failure.

It also demonstrates that most people that start a business do so because of a driving need or compelling vision that must be fully realized and highly successful, even if it means clinging to the side of a sinking ship, gulping water along the way.

What's particularly interesting to observe is, when Marcus sits down for an initial consultation to get their assessment of the issues, generally all the issues related to the failing business are attributed to the *operational* piece of the business. It's amazing how much money is lost in the process part of the business equation.

Here's the key insight however, (and definitely not lost on Marcus), the process is executed by humans – how they think, their emotions, their decision-making and behaviors which serves up the results. Yet, rarely do the business owners identify these elements as part of the problem (though some do suggest behavior as an issue, but usually of someone else, not theirs).

From the inception, many entrepreneurs and business owners are disconnected from the intricate role human behavior plays in starting and growing a successful business and how imperative it is to be keenly aware of how to work with it to get the best outcomes all along the way. They are not **"behavior literate"**. Building and running a successful

13

business requires special attention not only towards their own behavior, but to who they hire – beyond functional experience, specific skills and capabilities.

And here is where the breakdown can start to occur. Once you start hiring, you not only have to skillfully manage your own behavior, but also the behavior of those you lead -- continued growth, requires greater competency in behavior management.

What's been your experience? It's probable you've seen the range -- from highly skilled managers to those that are devoid of any sensitivity to the behavior happening around them.

Those brave souls from the show, who allow national exposure to their foibles, give us an opportunity to clearly see that every leader needs to be *behavior literate* -- skilled in working with human behavior and how it's expressed through skills, capabilities, personality, team interaction, and job performance. These are a leader's human resource. **It's more than just a department!** it is the imperative partner to your vision, business plan, strategy, processes and ultimately profits.

The purpose of this briefing then, is to assist you in working with this indispensable, critical part of your business success formula. It's an expanded companion to our first executive briefing *15 Shifts – The Essential Guide to Transform Your Talent Management.* 15 Shifts provides a broad overview. This publication provides an expanded discussion on the combination of several "shifts".

⇒ Shift #9: Employee training and development, in many cases, is misused and misunderstood and therefore its use must be changed

⇒ Shift #10: Talent management is about generating profitable behaviors

⇒ Shift #12: My talent management effectiveness can be measured. I can know how it's impacting my balance sheet

These "shifts" address areas in human resource/talent management, regarding strategy, planning and spending. They challenge antiquated thinking and practices that undermine business growth and value.

Show Me The Money! | JoAnn R. Corley | www.thehumansphere.com

It's this ongoing observation that compelled me to write this briefing. I see "money laying on the table", profits not realized. As you read, acting on even one tip or adopting one key insight could make a significant difference for your company, leadership effectiveness, profits and value.

> The most successful companies have behavior literate leaders. How can you tell?...by the decisions made regarding managing employees. And it's this leadership that will determine the overall value and profitability of a company.

An Important Note:
The Role of Leadership in Company Valuation

I have the great honor of being part of a business consulting community comprised of highly accomplished colleagues. They have provided millions of dollars of value to their clients over the years, one of whom is financial advisor Phil Symchych.

He works with companies to help them operate in a fiscally strategic way with an eye toward building wealth and company value. He counsels his clients and discusses in his book, *The Business Wealth Builders: Accelerating Business Growth, Maximizing Profits, and Creating Wealth*, that in order to do so, you must have an effective management and leadership team. He calls it "professionalizing management".

In fact, investing in leadership and management development, creating a formalized leadership and management infrastructure, increases a company's EBITDA (an estimate of company value based on earnings before interest, taxes, depreciation, and amortization). This is particularly important if you're building a business with the thought of selling.

Norman Brodsky, former owner of Citistorage and active business advisor to INC magazine, took this fact to heart. After first testing the market for buyers, he went to work to bolster areas of his business that would increase its value.

"Brodsky reformed the areas of his business that could pump up his multiple of EBITDA or purchase price. This meant taking care of contracts that were out of date and fortifying his management team. In the end the strategy worked: Brodsky sold CitiStorage in 2007 for 10 times the value of EBITDA."

Here is an expanded explanation:
http://www.inc.com/guides/2010/10/how-to-understand-earnings-or-ebitda.html

This theme is also becoming an emerging theme on Wall Street. Investors are seeing more and more, as in start-ups, that the quality of a management and leadership team, who they are, how they lead, matters when it comes to risking investment dollars and determining company value. When investing, you are doing so not just in a company product, service operation, but also in the qualities of those who are leading – the intangible components of the organization.

Many are realizing that financials alone do not provide the complete and needed picture for adequate risk assessment and are calling for financial reports to include intangibles. This phenomenon is characterized in several ways, Leadership Capital Index, leadership intangibles movement, and "value reporting disclosure" to name a few.

> **Value Reporting Disclosure**
"They propose a model they call "Value Reporting Disclosure" with enhanced business reporting where firms report information on business landscape (industry, technology trends, the political and regulatory environment, social, and environmental trends), strategy (mission, vision, goals, objectives, portfolio, governance), resources and processes (physical, social, organizational capital and key processes), as well as GAAP-based performance. By reporting these more intangible factors, they give investors better information for determining a firm's true value. Analysts perceive the benefits of better disclosure when they help long-term investors have greater confidence in future earnings." Source: *The Importance of Leadership Intangibles for Valuation*

Alan Freed & David Ulrich in a Harvard Business Review article described The Leadership Rating Index this way:

> **Leadership Rating Index**
"The leadership ratings index we have developed has two dimensions, or domains: individual and organizational. Individual refers to the personal qualities (competencies, traits, characteristics) of both the top leader and the key leadership team in the organization. Organizational refers to the systems these leaders create to manage leadership throughout the organization and the application of organization systems to specific business conditions." (HBR)

Each domain has 5 factors and is summarized as follows:

- Individual: Personal proficiency, strategist, executor, people manager, leadership differentiator

- Organizational: culture capability, talent management, performance accountability, information, work practices.

Both Accenture and Ernst & Young's Center for Business Innovation are working with these concepts as well.

"Accenture's finance and performance management group also reports that intangibles are an increasingly important part of a firm's value. Its classification of assets still includes monetary and financial assets, but also intangible assets of relationships, organization process, and human resources, and it proposes measures to track these intangible assets."

"Ernst & Young's Center for Business Innovation has also attempted to find out how investors use non-financial information in valuing firms. It concludes that non-financial criteria constitute, on average, 35% of an investor's decision. Sell-side analysts use non-financial data, and the more non-financial measures analysts use, the more accurate their earnings forecasts prove to be."

Imagine for a moment – 35% of a company's sense of value is based on the qualities, behaviors, and structure of its leadership/management team. What a thought!

For many companies, this is frightening! It's clear that Investors are wanting to become more behavior literate and are placing tremendous value on it. This is an essential imperative for leaders at all levels. It's also the key purpose of this briefing.

All of this centers around what's commonly known as the "soft skills" side of the business or what I call "the human element". (Soft skills - what an odd phrase. It's never made sense to me because in my experience, for many, soft skills are hard.)

|> Learn More

If you'd like to learn more here's a few recommended sites to start and from which the above quotes were taken noted with an *.

*The Importance of Leadership Intangibles for Valuation | SmartBrief
http://www.smartbrief.com/original/2016/01/importance-leadership-intangibles-valuation

**Calculating the Market Value of Leadership | Harvard Business Review *(complete explanation)*
https://hbr.org/2015/04/calculating-the-market-value-of-leadership

10 Leadership Elements that Maximize Business Value | Forbes
http://www.forbes.com/sites/martinzwilling/2015/11/03/10-leadership-elements-that-maximize-business-value/#36de18384990

Tangibles Over Intangibles
http://www.exinfm.com/board/intangibles_over_tangibles.htm

Taking Stock of Talent | Workforce
http://www.workforce.com/2016/01/27/taking-stock-of-your-talent/

The Leadership Capital Index: Realizing the Market Value of Leadership – David Ulrich

The Business Wealth Builders: Accelerating Business Growth, Maximizing Profits, and Creating Wealth, Phil Symchych

*"Human Resources isn't a thing we do.
It's the thing that runs our business."
– Steve Wynn, Wynn Las Vegas*

The Evolution of the Leadership Factor & Behavior Literacy

In the beginning...leading is easy...

a business was launched. The founder's intent, shaped through a vision and driving desire, was to provide a service or product that would meet the needs of hungry consumers. Simple plan – right?

In order for that vision to be successfully realized, 2 key components needed to be in place: *people and a process to produce and deliver those goods or services that would generate profits.*

From those humble beginnings, that simple vision, *if executed in an educated and strategic way,* could blossom into a wealth building resource for the founders and other participants. Whether launched from a kitchen table or a garage, it truly is a thrilling piece of the American dream!

In the beginning there was also no human resources department. The operational success or failure of a company was wholly dependent on the close relationship of the founders to its employees and customers. That relationship and employee experience shaped the company culture.

Here's my belief and observation – as companies grow, for many, that close interwoven employer/employee experience begins to unravel. External growth demands put pressure on internal processes, putting pressure on and take precedence over the employer/employee relational experience. An experience that is shaped by the personality, character, and values of the founders as well as their understanding of the role and needs of their human resource – their behavior literacy.

To be sure, without an applied understanding of the power of culture, relational leadership and human behavior, that unraveling may well be

19

taken for granted, perhaps minimized or excused and therefore go unattended with disruptive human consequences most likely to follow.

A great story that wonderfully demonstrates creating culture and leadership from individual values is Zappos. Pick up the book *Pursuit of Happiness: A Path to Profits, Passion and Purpose by Tony Hsieh and* you'll get a front row seat to their growth, Tony's leadership challenges, his intentional creation of culture derived from his core values in growing the company. Zappos was eventually bought by Amazon for $850 million dollars.

With growth comes the legitimate need for building an operational infrastructure – enter stage left -- the human resource department. In some cases, this process and subsequent use of can further alienate employees from key leaders and feel a bit dehumanizing further eroding the employee experience. It's as if the human part slowly diminishes in the context of operational needs.

As a company continues to grow, for some, key leaders become more and more entrenched in running and growing the business on the operational side and less and less connected to those helping them do so – the human side. They fail to develop behavior literacy or begin to lose their sensitivity to it. Their belief is, "Our people are being taken care of. That's what human resources is for and if there is a problem, they'll let us know." That sentiment reflects a blind spot to the power being abdicating that could be used to produce more of their desired results.

|> Leadership Insight

Leaders have great power they may not be using. And some, then blame their subordinates for not getting the results they themselves could be achieving.

Example: Did you know a random greeting and hand shake from an executive has tremendous motivating power for a lower level employee? It meets the human need of recognition, sense of worth and connection.

The reality is for many leaders; the evolution of growth can produce a greater distance from their employees. Oh they may work in the same building, but the emotional, psychological and spiritual connection is very thin or nonexistent. And for employees who enter a large company, opportunities to make connections with key leaders may not exist at all (and this is a need and desire of the new workforce becoming populated by millennials).

> Key leaders can become disconnected from or never connected to their most important resource -- their human resource...and how behavior impacts business operations. This disconnect impacts financial decisions.

No matter the size of a company, leaders who understand that connection and meaningful interaction (as recognized in *9 Smart Things the CEOs Do, INC.com*) within all levels are essential motivators for employees, that a sense of community is an important element of culture, make efforts to be present, communicate and find creative ways to nurture bonds, even if their only vehicle is technology.

They realize they have *unique power, via their position/title,* to express their vision, amplifying and demonstrate their company values and build an amazing culture to which talent will be attracted and gladly participate!

SIDE BAR | The Power of Your Leadership Brand...*it has value ($)*
Leadership Insight: Your brand contributes or undermines your company value.

The site Glassdoor conducts an annual survey scouring the corporate landscape for CEOs that are loved by employees and they are in a perfect position to do so. Their site allows employees to share their

unbridled opinions of their work experience, including what they think of their corporate leaders.

This is probably where some of the most truthful company intel can be found. It's also the go-to source where prospective talent can check out 'the real skinny" on an organization – at least from an employee's point of view. Have you checked for comments on your company lately?

It's also where we can gain useful insights regarding the value of a leader's brand. In the article, *Why Employees Love Their CEO*, here's an important point, "While customers and shareholders are important groups, a CEO has to please – if the employees don't respect their leader the business will ultimately suffer."

We could say there's a high probability this could impact the Leadership Index referenced earlier. CEOs and other senior leaders who understand this are demonstrating it by these simple activities and many more.

✓ Conducts regular town hall meetings, whether in person or by video
(My nephew, who works in Atlanta, experiences timely in-person town halls with Senior executives who are based in London. Yes, they fly in to be present and connect with all their teams in the U.S. Consider that some employees have never seen or met a senior leader and yet work in the same building or corporate campus.)

✓ Breakfast or lunch meetings
(Just when you think there is no time due to size, consider John Chambers, the CEO of Cisco Systems, who regularly has lunch with new hires.)

✓ After hours meet and greet
(The CEO of a former employer (ranked #1 on the INC list) at least once a quarter brought pretzels, chips and beer to our office on Friday for an informal meet & greet.)

✓ Is a built-in part of the on-boarding program
(Thomas Fanning, Southern Company, as I understand it, does not just stick his head in the door and say a few words, but presents several hours of on-boarding information.)

✓ Meeting 1/1 with every new hire
(This is a practice of Gary Vaynerchuk. If you've never heard of him, check him out. He is a unique leadership voice and force. Though many may not like his style, his impact and success cannot be denied

in business today.)

Being seen, present and genuinely attempting to connect is priceless! leadership capital with today's workforce. It sends a brand message to employees. Unfortunately, for many leaders, that capital, those brand shaping opportunities are freely and frivolously given away, in fact seen

---

My Observations

1. *Key leaders need to become more involved in relating to and managing their people at every level. When's the last time an entry level worker connected to, or had access to a C-suite executive or a top leader of the organization, whatever title they hold? There is great power there!*

2. *Average leaders (and old school leadership) lead by and from a company structure, restricting their connection and responsive to their "human resource" needs.*

---

as a burden, not an invaluable function. Yet it's critical for leaders who wish to position their companies as best in the marketplace.

For those leaders who are creatively responsive to the human needs outside their traditional structure, their companies tend to thrive (reference back to Zappos). Why? Because they fundamentally understand their leadership influence and power. They are behavior literate.

They also are keenly aware that **there are in fact 2 critical power sources in running and growing a successful business -- the power of the leader and the "power of the people".**

Without understanding, believing, and living this, companies will not competently manage their human resource nor realize their full potential and profits. They will continually work against themselves.

Toss untrained managers into the mix and there is a compounding affect. Many manage in a way that suppresses their "people power". That suppression is sometimes vented in ways that undermine needed outcomes. (There is a great example of this in the later part of this briefing.)

Many leaders know intellectually that the people part of the business, the role that employees play in a business' success is an essential element. Yet, because key leaders have become detached from or were never fully connected to this truth and the people they lead, either by experience, personal values, leadership philosophy, or lack of training, their employees are treated like a second string function. (Though many give substantial lip service otherwise).

Consequently, decisions related to people management are treated as such, sabotaging company goals, business strategy, and stifling profits. I call this "the big disconnect"!

That disconnect is most broadly reflected in how decision-makers choose to invest (or not) in meeting employees' needs and developing their capabilities. It reflects an additional leadership/management need that is an element of behavior literacy and that is financial literacy.

Though not in the traditional sense, this *financial literacy* is in the context of how behavior impacts profitability – determining the financial impact of behavior both positive and negative. This briefing also addresses this need with examples and exercises. In fact, we've designed this briefing to be a "learning/training" manual of sorts. You can conduct your own, or book an onsite facilitation.

Consider for a moment the definition of invest: *put money to use in something offering potential profitable returns; giving something to get something in return*. In the context of managing talent, when leaders are behavior and financially literate, this definition can be fully realized. Without it, the same kind of "we can't afford it", antiquated decision-making will continue to be replicated…undermining profit and growth.

> **|> 2 Important Insights**
>
> *1). Behavior and financial literacy is a new generation leadership/management competency.*
>
> *2). People Power = Profit Power*
> *People investment is company investment.*

What is People Power?

People power comprises 2 key elements:

1). The complete human make-up and attributes of an employee -- their "human resource".

2). What of those resources they choose to and/or are motivated to apply, to a job description, in any given moment to get needed results.

The chart on the following page, used in our leadership and management development initiatives, brings clarity to the definition.

Quick note: In the work we do, helping companies improve operational performance, we marry people power with results based leadership. Leadership that consciously works with people power is termed "human-centric".

When we say people or human, we mean their mind, heart, and spirit applied to their technical capability. We recognize and work with the complete human makeup, literally – and in doing so, term it holistic talent management.

**Activating and engaging these elements
is the most compelling leadership challenge today.**

Show Me The Money! | JoAnn R. Corley | www.thehumansphere.com

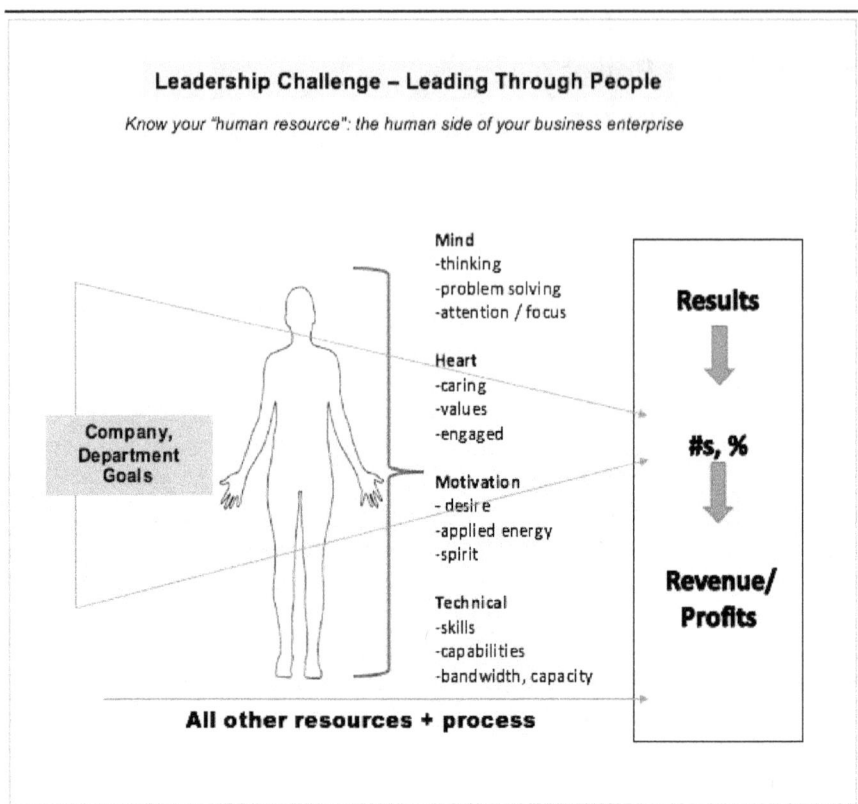

Leadership Challenge – Leading Through People

Know your "human resource": the human side of your business enterprise

Company, Department Goals

Mind
-thinking
-problem solving
-attention / focus

Heart
-caring
-values
-engaged

Motivation
- desire
-applied energy
-spirit

Technical
-skills
-capabilities
-bandwidth, capacity

All other resources + process

Results

⬇

#s, %

⬇

Revenue/ Profits

=> Look at this chart carefully… as a leader, how have you and every member of your leadership/management team impacted each element?

Let's pause for a moment.

Rarely does a leader have the opportunity to look at their "human resource" from such a literal perspective. However, it's imperative if a leader wants his/her company to become more successful.

What important truths, challenges and questions can be gleaned from viewing this chart? *Here are a few to consider:*

1. Human Resource, though a named function, department or profession, is actually the heart, mind, spirit and technical capabilities of an employee.

2. Many leaders are disconnected from this truth.

3. What kind of *leadership qualities* need to be in place to successfully connect with and activate these human elements?

4. These resources can be applied to process, strategy, other resources, and customer interaction to achieve needed business outcomes at any time in any measure (aka engagement) at *their* discretion! **Employees are in fact "business partners".** Many are not treated with that sense of value.

5. There are aspects of a company that can activate or *deactivate* these human elements (e.g. company culture, relationship with boss).

6. **Activation comes before engagement.**

7. These human resource components, if not effectively handled, can create operational bottlenecks, crippling your operational progress, growth, and profits. No matter the size of the bottleneck, it slows down or blocks desired outcomes.

8. Without competent leadership and management timely addressing these bottlenecks *(being behavior literate),* they will become a characteristic part of your operation and company culture, ensuring a negative impact to long term growth.

9. Those closest to working with these critical human recourses (hearts, minds, spirits, technical capabilities) are typically front line supervisors and managers who commonly get the least amount of training and/or support. (Hum…this is scary.)

10. Related to #9, if a traditional corporate structure is to remain, there needs to be a hyper focused commitment to build management/supervisory capabilities to mitigate "mis-management" of this crucial resource.

11. We can safely conclude: **It's common for companies to entrust their most important asset to their least experienced.**

12. Business strategy needs to include how to continually activate, engage and grow the mind, heart, spirit, and technical capabilities of every employee, believing and demonstrating that "people growth is business growth". We could also say, "If you're not growing your people, it would be difficult to really grow your business." **Your business can only grow to the capability of those who run the business.**

13. **People power is the power to make or break your business!** How are your leaders working/leveraging/collaborating with this power?

14. If key leaders do not embrace these human truths, your company will be incapable of reaching its potential.

In considering the chart, what additional observations, insights or conclusions can you draw -- keeping in mind…your leadership philosophy, practices, business planning & strategy, committed and deployed financial resources, leadership/management development, company culture, employee rewards & recognition programs?...to name a few.

 Essential Question: How behavior literate is your leadership and management team?...financially literate?

Literacy defined: someone who is educated in a specific area of knowledge.

Better Business Building

#1 Leverage Your People Power: Know where you are, where you want to go and how you're going to get there…and lead in such a way people willingly follow, applying all of their human resource.

For most of you reading this, that directive is not new information. However, as you continue, see it through a fresh lens by keeping in mind the human chart on the previous page.

As a company continues to grow, the leadership and management team **is <u>the</u> key** to continually unlocking, activating, engaging and growing the human resource to meet and take on increased needs. (And by the way, for those of you who have one, this is <u>*not*</u> the ultimate responsibility of the human resource department. They should be playing a support role*, not the key role.*)

Some leaders assume because folks are employed they will automatically and willingly follow and everyday bring to bear their "human resource". But many others know this is not true. We've learned that we have to be the kind of leaders and *create the kind of conditions* (relationship and culture) that will encourage and inspire this to happen vs. discourage and suppress.

> *To met the needs of the current employee population (from all generations) human-centered leadership is the kind of leadership that is now required and to which **all employees** will be the most responsive!*

So what results will **your** "human resource" be rallied to achieve? It's up to you, your key leaders and managers to continually review and *obsessively communicate. (There's a funny thing about results – we always get them; they just may not be the ones we want.)*

Observation: Yes, I did use the word obsessively. I've observed expectations are not communicated enough. Follow one of the many "abcs" of leadership – always be communicating! Just because it's in your head, doesn't mean it's in theirs. There are way too many distractions that keep employees unfocused. **Leaders must doggedly capture and re-direct that focus. Focus is a human resource.**

Additionally, here's where the skill, the leadership capability of *aligning, connecting, engaging* the human resource to process and strategy for desired outcomes must be in place. Again, this is not the core function of the HR department. It is lead and driven everyday by those who manage and lead on the front lines. The HR department's role is to support that – not be responsible for it. In many companies, this is reversed, which severely undermines the influence and leadership development of direct reports.

Aligning, connecting, engaging is commonly accomplished through job performance management. (We make this much easier through our results based leadership framework). Effective leadership (aka performance management) includes all of the above including *collaborative feedback.*

We see collaborative feedback not as one-way (top-down) and not only as two-way, **but additionally "top around"**. All decision-makers and participants should be included in cyclical feedback that continually improves anything that can bolster results, creating a team and company culture that reflects the sense that we're all in this together, everyone is contributing and every voice matters.

Remember, in the beginning when there was no human resource department, this element of management, utilizing people power was done naturally and informally. The real-time interaction prompted on going "training and development". Employees' capabilities and contributions evolved in the context of what was needed by the business in serving the customer.

Today, I think we have over-formalized many of the early employer/employee experiences that create no real value and seem to be a distraction and complicate operations. There is robust, ongoing debate in the human resource/talent management community regarding this – for example, highly structured performance management.

Making good decisions is a crucial skill at every level.
-Peter Drucker

| HR Side Bar

Over the many years of being in this profession here is something I've observed: The human resource and talent management industry has turned needed leadership competencies into independent HR department functions...and it's being allowed because leaders aren't doing them, don't know how to do them or don't see them as a crucial piece of their role. In some cases, it's to the point of ridiculous.

Here's 2 Examples

Example A: High structured performance management - appraisals: can you imagine in the startup days if an employee was only given periodic feedback on their performance/contribution. The business could not run! An employee's performance was intricately entwined in the operations. (Our fancy term is "strategically aligned".) Feedback was a natural function and continuously given regarding the employee's contribution in the context of the immediate needs of the business.

What do we do now? Let's tell them in 3 months what they did 3 months ago or even 6 months or a year ago...about a set criterion of which sometimes neither the manager or team member feel has any direct connection to the business. For some it feels random and irrelevant.

This is not to say that formal performance management is not needed, it's more about the way it's set-up and executed. No matter your stance on *formal performance management*, <u>strategic performance management -- handling and directing the day-to-day contribution of employees -- needs to be in place</u>, ideally in a natural, collaborative way.

Consider it simple, low tech ongoing feedback – let's call it a process conversation (with a sprinkling of appreciation and recognition tossed in), which is a common function of coaching, leading and managing goals. Employees consistently need to know how they're doing in relation to needed results. It's timely accountability and an important element of running a successful business – *not* a separate HR function.

It's also a motivator. Goal setting and feedback is one of many ways to activate and engage the mind, heart, and spirt of an employee and is also part of our framework for results based leadership. Our framework takes into account every aspect of the "human resource" we've been discussing, in conjunction with the science of human behavior.

Example B: A leadership/management training (workshop, seminar or e-learning module) on how to motivate employees: This is a very common practice – have a workshop or seminar on this type of topic without a strategic plan to integrate it into the day-to-day activities of the leader, with the thought that in doing so, the leader will better meet operational objectives. Without tying it to strategic objectives, it's treated as an independent function and seen as a nice thing to do, without any meaningful connection.

Again, it is my observation that many leaders are abdicating their leadership responsibilities to an HR department and therefore undermining operational effectiveness and suppressing leadership and management development. In the beginning...the was no HR department.

#2 Measuring Matters
It's Difficult to Effectively Manage What You Do Not Measure
What are you measuring?

An additional element to successful business building is measuring and tracking. We automatically do this financially, though my colleague Phil Symchych says that could be improved with *creating current, real time, daily data* vs. post view (*example:* financial reporting for the previous month not available until the 10th). He calls that looking back -- that's where we were, but where are we now?

"The most useful financial information shows exactly where you are now and where you are going to be in the near future, just like a good navigation system in your car."

Symchych, Phil; Weiss, Alan (2015-10-06). The Business Wealth Builders: Accelerating Business Growth, Maximizing Profits, and Creating Wealth

Similar to financials, and in the spirit of strategic human resource management, including performance alignment, it's useful to have real-time performance indicators reflecting the activity and experiences of managers and employees (keeping in mind the literal interpretation of human resource - heart, spirit, mind & technical capabilities).

For example, common in manufacturing, "KPIs" (key production indicators) are used. What is not so common is a twist on "KPIs" and that is **"key people indicators"**.

To do this, top leaders need to determine what they want to measure on the human side of the enterprise. These should be tied to and a compliment of company values and intended company culture. Determining and then measuring the human side in this way is also another element of behavior literacy.

Some companies use of KPIs as key performance indicators, applied primarily to leaders and managers. "Key people indicators" suggest that leaders need to keep their finger on the pulse, more literally the "power level" of their employees reflected in the state of their mind, heart, spirit and technical capabilities.

Here's some starter questions to ask…

➢ What would you like to continually measure or track to ensure your human resource is functioning at its best and being effectively managed?

➢ What do you need to monitor to avoid escalation of troublesome employee issues?

These are important questions! My client work has generated an interesting list of items leaders want to track – all of which are related to the mind, heart, spirit, and technical capabilities of their human resource and which also are a reflection of the direct impact and effectiveness of supervisors and managers.

- trust
- respect
- appreciation

- rapport / relations
- recognition
- happiness
- engagement
- skill development / training (what's the plan? – the EDP/employee development plan)
- supervisor, team lead, manager impact

In essence, these reflect qualities and company culture descriptors that activate, grow and motivate their "human" resource. The lack of these can adversely impact your people power. They influence the willingness of employees to use / offer their resources – even beyond what's needed or requested. This is called discretionary offering and is quite ideal!

These KPIs are really a way of measuring the employee experience. They amplify and strengthen the practice of strategic human resource management.

Some companies do measure in some ways, an example of which is the use of formal employee surveys in a variety of forms – usually conducted once a year or every 2 years. This infrequency can be troublesome, however, because it's essential information received too late. Perhaps these would best be used to benchmark current conditions and then used as a follow-up once issues have been addressed, thus creating a before and after picture.

The *Great Place to Work group* measures trust. They are doing extraordinary work in helping companies create human-centered cultures and leadership. The companies that espouse to this approach are thriving. You can learn more about them here. https://www.greatplacetowork.com/   Their offerings are a fresh approach to a traditional employee survey.

What we've discovered in the use of our results based leadership, which includes built in accountability to employee activity and utilizes multiple activators and engagement practices, is that we are *constantly attuned* to the quality of the employee experience. And, if there are any concerns, they can be quickly addressed. This leadership framework in and of itself is a monitoring mechanism.

Leadership Question: How much time & money could be saved if employee issues were quickly and adequately addressed?

> **|> Leadership Insight**
>
> 1. Tracking the human/employee experience is equally as important as tracking sales, production or revenue.
>
> 2. What you track you can quickly address and manage.

But no matter what you use, the key point is to actively monitor the human/employee experience as you would any other part of the business.

Tracking the vital signs of your human resource would be a radical change for many companies and yet is sorely needed! ...and would save a boatload of money. Some wait until the team members are on life support before any action is taken – and for others, it's too late. Their talent has left.

 **The Power of Daily**

In Phil's' book *The Business Wealth Builders*, referenced earlier, he shares an important insight and practice, "The best way to improve performance in a critical area is to report on that performance every day, compare good days vs. bad days, and continually share what is working on the good days to **ensure that all days keep getting better.**"

He suggests using daily 'flash reports". "Flash reports tell you where you are, in real time, every day and can be used in any aspect of the business. Flash reports, related to employee performance (if used constructively), can empower employees to measure and improve their performance."

What a great universal best practice – *ensure all days keep getting better*, while also fostering an enjoyable, healthy performance culture.

In applying this philosophy to every aspect of business operations, imagine the acceleration of revenue. It's really a take on "the slight edge rule", which I term the 1% edge. If you can improve by 1% a day, you can double your effectiveness in 70 days. The power of this approach is a constant, fixed and realistic view of improvement.

> *"I used to think business was 50 percent having the right people.*
> *Now I think it's 80 percent."*
> *Kevin P. Ryan – Internet Entrepreneur*

GAME CHANGER

So, imagine having KPIs, key people indicators, and applying this practice.

What would be the benefit of having current information on the condition (the human qualities/aspect) of your teams on a regular basis?... vs. the common practice of waiting until something troublesome surfaces? Just like we monitor the vitality or optimum functionality of the components in our cars, you can monitor the same of your people power. **Monitoring, check-ups, and tune-ups** are valuable practices for the human side of your enterprise.

Through determining and monitoring your key people indicators, you can <u>progressively strengthen</u> your human resource performance, capabilities, and capacity as the company continues to grow. It's proactive talent management vs. reactive.

Key Questions: How much money do you think this approach and practice could save? How could it impact your bottom line? Which best describes your people management – proactive or reactive? You can probably surmise that those leaders with high behavior & financial literacy are proactive.

A Leadership Observation

It's a common occurrence...

A team is not getting along. There is interdepartmental rivalry. Just about every employee has or will experience this in their work-life time.

Some go on for long periods of time and become a characteristic part of a company's culture. All of this is most commonly described as the inability to manage conflict.

This is a significant *leadership handicap*. It's uncommon to find a leader who skillfully manages conflict. Most don't and in fact avoid it, relinquishing the impact to – well whatever.

I've consistently seen that a very popular reason a team gets to a place of life support is due to unresolved conflict and/or hidden resentments…and the leader is no help (which actually adds to the resentment). This is not only an emotional intelligence issue, but a behavior literacy issue as well.

- ➲ What would be the value to you if, embedded in your company culture, was the ability for employees, at any level to successfully manage conflict?
- ➲ What would you be willing to pay to achieve this outcome?
- ➲ What would be the return-on-investment if you did?
- ➲ If this is a current challenge within your organization, what's it costing you?
- ➲ What's the ripple effect?

Tip: Have every team create a conflict management protocol.

On a Personal Note
Over the years, I have delivered thousands of professional development workshops and seminars, addressing a variety of "topical" needs. After all this time and thousands of workshops later, I can confidently say, there is a lot of money wasted here. Seminar companies have trained the uneducated to attempt to solve problems by workshop titles – in many cases applying a band-aid when surgery is really required.

In the end, (and this is the result of becoming behavior literate) there are a just a few core capabilities every employee needs to have. When developed, they impact and/or address all other performance needs. Managing conflict is one – click here to see the others. Top employee competencies Advice: invest in meaningful solutions vs. buying topic titles.

Summary of Leadership Imperatives

(here's just a few from our reading so far...)

⇒ See your "human resource" differently.

⇒ Commit to fostering competent managers.

⇒ Lead in a way that it's clear your employees are partners and treat them as such.

⇒ Stay connected to every level of employee, their needs and point of view.

⇒ Expect behavior and financial literacy for all leaders and managers.

Become an Expert Human Resource Manager
Every leader needs to be one.
It's not a department, but a leadership / management competency.

As you've been reading, when you encounter the words "human resource" hopefully, you're now seeing it from a fresh perspective and more literal form. I'm also hoping you've gained a greater understanding of the role this resource plays in achieving the outcomes you desire for your company.

Another essential element in effective human resource management is to be clear on the connection between your human resource and revenue.

The specific human elements we've discussed (mind, heart, spirit) manifest into behaviors that produce results wanted or unwanted. Those results can be translated into money. *We call them profitable or unprofitable behaviors.*

That's why its so important for leaders to clearly understand the financial impact behavior plays. Human behavior is either serving profits or not. This understanding is sorely lacking, otherwise <u>behavior would be taken more seriously.</u> This is the spirit of behavior literacy.

To help you tune into behavior, let's start with a few questions to ask yourself and your leadership team:
- ? What would you consider to be profitable behaviors?
- ? Unprofitable behaviors?
- ? What behaviors do you want?
- ? What behaviors are currently undermining results?
- ? What behaviors are clearly costing you?
- ? What questions would you add?

Some companies have answered a few of these questions and identified them as behavior competencies. For sure, answers to these questions could help managers and supervisors lead with more precision, when they are integrated into daily performance management.

Ultimately its clear -- *human resource management (behavior management) is business management.*

It cannot and should not be relegated to a department alone, treated like an 2nd class function, if a business is to fully and successfully execute it's plans and achieve operational goals. Instead, it should be an integral part of business planning, strategy, operational monitoring and financial investment.

And for those companies that do have a fully functioning HR department, that department should be an integral part of all business planning, decisions and activities supporting the leadership vs. replacing it!

And here is where we've come full circle. Earlier I shared a condition and phrase I termed "the big disconnect.'

Earlier:
    "The people part of the business, the role that employees play in a business' success is an essential element. Yet, because leaders have become detached to or were never fully connected to this truth or the employees either by experience, personal values, or leadership philosophy, it's treated as a second string function.

    Consequently, decisions related to people management are treated as such, undermining company goals, business strategy and stifling profits. I call this "the big disconnect"!

Many leaders are unplugged
from their most important resource
…a resource that drives the success of their company – or not.

A Deeper Dive
Developing Behavior Literacy
Connecting to the Human Element – Working with Intangibles

Why do we struggle so much in working with this side of our company operations? Why is it easy to become disconnected as previously mentioned?

The main reason I believe is it's an intangible (and I think the phrase "soft skills" is a derivative of this). It's the dilemma we discussed when applying value to Leadership via a leadership index. It's trying to make something concrete that is not.

Yet it's a leadership imperative. Leaders must connect to the fact that intangibles can cost or bring value – that behavior has a financial impact. In fact, *it's the intangibles that have the greatest impact to a company's profitability.*

✓ Consider the intangibles as critical. Intangibles are powerful indicators of the health of a business, team, fit of an employee, or competency of a manager.

✓ Intangibles can guide leaders to areas that need special attention, improvement or can identifying best practices – it's another way to describe KPIs – key people indicators.

✓ Intangibles also impact company valuation.

These are key elements of behavior and financial literacy.

What Are Intangibles?

Intangible defined: An intangible is non physical in nature. Examples of intangibles include: corporate intellectual property, such as patents, trademarks, business methodologies, brand recognition, leadership qualities, employees with specific skills, etc.

Intangibles tend to reside on and are sourced from the human side of the enterprise. Additional examples include morale, work satisfaction, positive atmosphere, or creative culture and is defined as unable to touch or grasp – yet known as present. We can see it or feel it though we are not able to touch it.

For many company leaders, intangibles are given little attention and yet are crucial to business success. They run companies, connect to strategy and process. They in fact drive outcomes. They need their keen attention. Every leader needs to know which matter to them and their business, which need attention more and which need attention less.

As you continue through this briefing, give special attention to the theme of intangibles and the role they play because...intangibles lead to tangibles and as related to our title, that is money.

To follow are 2 examples of the role intangibles play – 1 from the employee performance side and one from the leadership/decision-maker's side.

> A client recently said (as he was experiencing an 'ah-ha" moment in a leadership development initiative),
>
> **"If we manage the intangibles better, the tangibles will come."**

Note: At the end of this briefing are 2 examples/case studies of how taking care of the intangibles via leadership and management development were translated into a tangible, measureable financial impact. One of them was a powerful department transformation.

Examples of Intangibles
As a practicing founder of The Human Sphere, I have the privilege and opportunity to work with clients and their employees at every level. The next two pieces discuss the human or intangible side of business operations. When a leader asks, "Where should we look to improve our outcomes?" We recommend look to the human side first. It's typically *not* the first place leaders go.

What's Holding Back Your Company May Not Be What You Think

Leading and running a business can be a daunting endeavor no matter the size, even running a department or team for that matter can seem like a formidable challenge. The pressure is ever present to deliver results and for some, knowing how to improve results is the ultimate leadership test.

If you have not been getting the outcomes you want or wish to improve what's already a decent operation, there might be some "human elements" to consider that are undermining your business performance. The human element or human performance is commonly overlooked in considering profitable improvements.

It's not the first place many leaders and business owners consider and yet it's a key component to quickly impact improved results. What's initially considered in the quest to enhance results is other resources and processes (sales & marketing, strategy & planning for example), rather than the "human resource". Part of behavior literacy is knowing that's a place to look.

This is not to say those areas should not be reviewed. It's just common that human performance is not in the mix or weighted as a critical piece.

Performance management (talent management) is business management -- successful business management must include talent/performance management.

And...it should start with the leader and or leadership team. Even if human performance is considered, leaders don't typically look at themselves first and ask questions such as, "What about me and my leadership has allowed this to be or has lead us to where we are now or not?"

So even if you just need to fine tune your results, here is a list of common human elements to look for that impact performance. You can apply this list to both you and your teams. (Also consider this list a contribution to your behavior literacy.)

Qualities or conditions that adversely impact human performance, undermine effectiveness, productivity and ultimately could be holding back your business (starter list):

- confusion
- lack of clarity of what to do, or what is wanted
- saying yes too much
- not saying no enough
- overwhelm
- fear
- lack of process (the tangible, executable road map)
- lack of courage
- not communicating frequently enough
- last of trust
- broken rapport with team members
- not communicating clearly
- keeping and or not addressing toxic employees
- inability to prioritize
- pushing too hard
- pushing too little
- leadership vacuum
- lack of boundaries
- discouragement

- lack of relevant knowledge
- unresolved hurts
- arrogance
- minimal appreciation
- micro-managing
- disrespect
- lack of focus
- absence of accountability

I'm confident in saying that if someone asked a leader, "What's holding back your business?", the items on this list would probably not be mentioned or be top of mind and yet one of these effectively addressed could unlock better outcomes and profits.

Here's an important question, "Do you truly believe addressing any of these will impact your profits?" I ask that, because though many leaders say yes to that question, they don't act or make decisions in a way that reflects that. This is a sure indicator they really don't believe it. Actions reflect beliefs and inaction reflects beliefs.

For example, if you as a leader have struggled with any of these for an extended period time and have not gotten help, that suggests there is a belief (probably subconscious) that it's not important, it doesn't matter and it's really not relevant to the bigger picture -- that it's not impacting the business outcomes you value and desire.

Many leaders function with a perilous insensitivity to how the human experience in their company environments impacts business outcomes. This is a leadership hazard that must be remedied. Without doing so, the human resource of a company will be perpetually misused and underutilized. (Side note: some would classify this sensitivity under the umbrella of emotional and social intelligence.)

In my experience, getting help and effectively addressing these doesn't have to be a full blown science experiment. Perhaps seeing it as such is what holds decision-makers back from seeking assistance.

Coaching tip: Develop an awareness and understanding of how specific areas of the human element impacts your business outcomes. If there are certain areas you believe need improvement, ask the team members in that area what's going on and what would be required to achieve new goals. You may very well discover that what's needed is related to some or many of the conditions listed above. Then create KPIs around those needs to monitor improvements over time.

Questions:

⇒ *Do you know which of those listed are present in your company, department, team and to what degree?*

⇒ *Depending on measure (to what degree), do you know how much it's costing you (the company)... how it's impacting revenue?*

Your answer is important – one in which decision-makers must be clear. Because, when you're presented with the opportunity to achieve even a fraction of the list through investing in the knowledge, development and growth of your "human resource", yet tempted to use a common response that habitually reverberates through-out our corporate landscape, "We can't afford it," it would be to your advantage and that of your company's balance sheet to be clear on...

> which intangibles are the most meaningful to you
> which of these does your company need the most
> what would you be willing to pay for them and
> what's the cost to you and your company if any of these are absent.

|> Decision Insight

Many HR professionals & decision-makers choose a "training", workshop or seminar to address the needs mentioned above only to find that alone is not sufficient to adequately do so. In creating a plan, be clear on what you're investing in and what you want and what the operation needs in outcomes. A combination of options is proving to provide the best return.

For example, in general, a training is generic, while coaching is specific and customized with accountability for a duration of time. *A seminar is informational while coaching is developmental and can be transformational.*

A day in a training classroom vs. addressing needs via peer/group coaching for a period may be the better option, which can integrate both.

Additionally, when a person or group is underperforming, coaching provides accelerated results in restoring and improving a meaningful return when considering ROI and return-on-compensation.

Similar to earlier advice: If you need development, don't buy a product, invest in outcomes.

Another interesting side of a business that is not given much attention is the leadership experience. After returning from a debrief, I was moved to write this.

Leaders Have Feelings Too

It had been an exciting 8 weeks! A new leadership-management training/development initiative had been launched -- the format of which was something new, never tried before. Everyone agreed it was a risk.

After years of attempting to effectively "train" managers and leaders using traditional approaches (the results of which left everyone wanting), it was time to embrace fresh thinking and a new approach. It was time to jump off the insanity train. (You know, doing the same thing over and over but expecting different results.)

As I sat across from the President and Human Resource Director of this very busy, multimillion dollar manufacturing concern for our final debrief, I was aware that the experiment was a success, how much and to want degree I had yet to learn.

Of course what I wanted to see and hear most was how the success of the leadership and management changes in that short 8 weeks had impacted their daily, weekly and monthly numbers and the ultimate impact to their bottom line. But the discussion that unfolded went surprisingly a different direction.

The President began, "We can talk about the numbers, JoAnn, but there is a story to tell here." He then went on to share story after story about the direct and substantial impact to specific people, how they behaved differently, their change in attitude. One manager in particular few people liked but was now being nominated by multiple people for an award."

I eased back in my chair continuing to listen, more intently now, to the duet of stories they sung. I assumed when we arranged this debrief meeting that numbers were going to be the driving theme -- increased profits, better percentages of productivity, product and money saved. Yet, that was not at all the most compelling elements of our discussion. It was the impact to their employees -- the human impact.

I was schooled that day on the deeper impact of the work I do. You'd think I'd know this since my company is named The Human Sphere were we champion the human side of business enterprise, carrying the belief that when employees are winning the company wins too! Yet, in working with many decision-makers, numbers drive the decisions and measurement of our engagement success.

On this day, the human side of our successful work shone through for the employees and the leaders. And this was my most significant "ah-ha" reminder. As they enthusiastically shared more results, I gained deeper clarity that the work was as much for the human needs of the leaders as it was for their employees.

When we talk about doing work "for an organization"...what we're really addressing is meeting the operational needs as well as the human needs -- all the humans of the organization, leaders included. Though some leaders may not wish to acknowledge this, human needs and operational needs are inseparable partners to the success of any company.

Here's what human needs of the leaders I heard...

- I feel relieved - so glad this experiment worked
- I want to meet the needs of my employees, but didn't exactly know how
- I am so happy that they are happy and productive
- I needed to be open to something different and so glad I was
- I feel successful as a leader because I brought help that worked
- I feel good about what has occurred
- I was tired of feeling frustrated
- The state of our staff really matters to me
- I was bothered by what was not working
- I don't like to see my employees suffer and struggle
- I'm so glad they feel better equipped to manage certain challenges

- It's a great feeling the plant culture is significantly improved
- It's wonderful to see certain employees empowered and effective
- I'm so proud of the progress
- I am confident in our continued success
- I appreciate the help -- we needed it

... this is just a start.

Thanks to this client, I've been reminded that leaders, decision-makers are very human, with intrinsic needs they may not wish to display. Some see certain leaders as "heartless." For those I see (for whatever the reason) a heart perhaps wounded, less activated, engaged or connected to those they lead.

For many, being vulnerable is considered a liability not an asset. There's little accolades for leaders who admit, "I'm afraid, I'm overwhelmed, I don't have a clue what do do, I'm at a loss, I need help." Instead, those emotional states are usually unconsciously masked by counterproductive behaviors, confusing leadership and diminished or handicapped performance.

Here's meaningful advice for any leader, "Give yourself permission to acknowledge I have needs and if I do, my staff probably does as well. Meeting their needs is meeting my needs...and that's ok."

All the above can be summarized with one final observation. It was clear that these 2 leaders felt good and happy about the success of the engagement because they genuinely cared about their employees -- not just what they could produce for the company, but their state as human beings.

In leadership, management consulting and HR, we work a lot with a variety of leadership competencies lists. I've yet to see listed "genuinely care about those you lead". Now I have seen empathy, an element of emotional intelligence, but simply put -- caring for the people you lead will payoff in unimaginable ways.

Think about it...what does caring do, what role does it play in certain contexts? One thing for sure, it drives and influences decisions. You can tell if, how much or what someone cares about by the decisions they make.

Now all leaders care about something... from profits to getting things done to being the best in a category. Be clear, what is most cared about is what will be the priority, drive how one leads, and influence how money is spent.

With regards to caring about employees, many leaders claim they care, but their decisions don't reflect it. What leaders most care about is where they will put their time, attention, passion and financial resources. Here's a great example -- Marriott's employee health and wellness initiative:

How Marriott Dominated the Hotel Industry By Focusing On Employee Health And Wellness https://t.co/dqCwakEh7O — Jacob Morgan (@jacobm) January 6, 2016

It's clear that acknowledging and meeting the needs of the human side of business enterprise carries huge benefits for all parties -- both internal and external customers.

As leaders, perhaps it's time to more readily admit we have needs and feelings too. I think connecting with our own humanity bolsters our leadership effectiveness overall and ultimately the success of our companies.

Final Note: I purposely included these 2 blog posts to offer examples to share the power of intangibles and the impact on you and your organization. In reality, since we're all human – these are universal. It's really about how many, which ones specifically, are most meaningful at any given moment and to what degree.

Note: Whether we realize it or not, as leaders, there *is* a personal cost when the needs of employees are not met. From stress to leadership credibility and decreased engagement – there is an impact. (I think if leaders were more aware, decisions would be different).

"When people go to work, they shouldn't have to leave their hearts at home."
-Betty Bender

So What is The Big Disconnect?

It's safe to summarize, from our previous section, that many leaders are disconnected and not tuned into their human resource -- the tremendous people power at their disposal and therefore are not utilizing it to its full potential – in fact lack behavior and financial literacy.

This disconnect can be derived from and reflected as follows:

1. A fundamental lack of knowledge of how people operate (what human beings need to be at their best).
2. Not seeing human behavior from an operational perspective, e.g. productive or unproductive (other descriptors "profitable or costly")…and therefore not taking it seriously.
3. Inability to measure the financial impact of those behaviors.
4. Inability to determine the return on and value of investing in performance and developmental needs of employees.

It is my belief that *every leader*, or as I call them in the book *15 Shifts* "talent management practitioner/human resource manager", needs to be well versed in understanding these 4 elements. Like bookkeepers who need to know basic accounting to successfully execute their role, the same holds true for those who are responsible for leading and running companies and therefore by default managing their talent.

This knowledge is so critical to maximizing a company's success and profits, I felt compelled to write about it resulting in the book, *15 Shifts: An Essential Guide to Transform Your Talent Management*. In retrospect, I think the title should have been, Transform Your Talent Management --Transform Your Profits. That book provides a broad, operational, and holistic view of talent management. The purpose of

51

this briefing is to expand discussion and understanding surrounding the financial impact of talent/human resource management – to improve behavior/financial literacy.

The 4 elements of disconnect presents an interesting decision-making dilemma. As I meet with leaders, it is very common for them to decline getting help or invest in tools and resources that could <u>profitably</u> impact staff performance. **They in fact decide against their own self interest and ultimately their company's revenue.** The disconnect serves as blinders.

Shocking I know. In my experience, no matter the size of a company or level of leadership, this decision-making scenario is pervasive.

This is where we suggest you take a moment to see where your decisions, thought, and actions lie in relation to the 4 elements of disconnect.

This is critical to the use of the remaining information.

Though the elements of the disconnect is a significant problem, it's what the disconnect produces that is most harmful -- the crippling by-product of *irrational fear*.

Lack of knowledge fuels fear. That fear greatly influences decision-making, creating emotional and mental shackles, producing decisions that undermine many needs of multiple stakeholders. The most prominent fear is wasting money.

Additionally, the 4 elements of disconnect feeds a belief and common practice that addressing human resource needs is a cost rather than an investment and therefore, if money has not been allocated or budgeted, it's money that can't be spent.

As you continue to read, we'll provide 3 solutions addressing each of the disconnects, which will help you and your leadership team develop a fresh perspective from which to make better decisions to support vs. undermine the outcomes you desire and need.

The 3 solutions will help you...

1. Learn to see, tune into, read and track the impact of behavior.

2. Learn to identify and lead from the attributes and behaviors that are most needed for your companies' success. This feeds into any formal performance management.

3. Learn to calculate the financial impact of behavior.

4. Learn to see money differently to achieve greater operational and financial results.

The above serve as a practical breakdown of what it means to be behavior literate. When applied, it will help you effectively work with your people power in a way that will grow your leadership effectiveness and value, business revenue and company value.

"Before you are a leader, success is all about growing yourself.
When you become a leader, success is all about growing others."
~ Jack Welch

Solution #1: Adjust Your View – Learn to see & read behavior
See beyond the person, it's behaviors you're looking for…

I was talking with a client recently about the talent of a certain team. We both agreed they were certainly a talented bunch.

Well, what exactly did we mean? Could we specifically identify what talented meant?

As mentioned earlier, the ability to identify behaviors (this is beyond just looking at skills) is an essential part of human resource – talent management. And so it's useful to ask again, "Do you see behaviors as a resource? How do you view and assess your "human resource"?"

These kinds of questions, with continued use, help leaders and key decision-makers become skilled at **operational talent management –** aligning behavior to operations.

Beyond the questions from the previous sections, as an exercise, let's apply this to your leadership team and conduct a low-tech assessment.

 *Keeping in mind your leadership team, answer the following:*

"What behaviors do your leadership and/or management team need to successfully execute your company's processes and strategy."

Which behaviors, qualities, and attributes would you list?

The list you create is what we'll call your "profitable behaviors". They support and drive process and strategy to achieve your revenue goals.

NOW...Identify & Assess

Again, considering your leadership team, continue:

1. How is each member of your team doing with each behavior on your list? (to what degree or measure, e.g. scale 1-5?) Do you see them demonstrated?
2. What is the value of each behavior to the organization?
3. Are there some behaviors on your list more valuable to you than others (more weighted)?
4. How do these behaviors impact, contribute to revenue/profitability and other aspects of the business?

Note: To broaden the view of performance, replace the word behavior with qualities or attributes.

Now explore the opposite.

1. What behaviors do your leaders / managers possess that undermine process and strategy? (I call them "behavior bottlenecks".)
2. With these behaviors in mind, what is the *ripple effect* or collective impact to your company starting with the team, department, etc.?
3. How is revenue being impacted?
4. What is it costing you, team, department, company – tangibly and intangibly?...it's important to identify both.
   (For intangible you can reference the section *What's Holding Back Your Company?*)
5. What is the short term impact?...long term impact?
6. Is there any legal exposure?*

*Legal exposure needs to be a standard, strategic consideration and takes many company leaders by surprise in the following areas: sexual harassment, bullying, intimidation, hostile work environment, discrimination.

This list, related to Federal employment laws, can have severe financial consequences. Of special note is bullying, intimidation and hostile work environment. It is worth it to help every manager/leader see what this legally looks like.

Of course if you're focused on building the kind of company culture we've been discussing, these issues would only relate to a rouge few vs. a common characteristic. None the less, be vigilant and make sure that there is a "no tolerance" policy for these behaviors or company culture characteristics!

Ensure there are adequate processes in place for reporting that can be swift and thorough, so that issues can be remedied quickly.

Creating Your Impact Map
You have to see the big picture to make the best decisions.

The first element in addressing Solution #1 was working through the above exercise -- to read the behavior of your management team and assess the financial impact. You were asked to use 2 simple activities -- answer questions and apply a 1-5 rating. In partnership with these two, the next step is to create your impact map.

An **impact map** is charting *the ripple effect* of a situation or incident and can be done in the same style as a mind map. What needs to be charted?

> *Here's a few considerations to start:*
> ✓ The point of initiation – where it started
> ✓ Who has been impacted? – to what degree?
> ✓ What has been impacted? – to what degree?
> ✓ How far reaching is it? (…to what departments, customers)
> ✓ For how long?
> ✓ What's the immediate financial effect?
> ✓ What's the potential long term financial effect?
> ✓ Is there any legal exposure – if so what?

Also, it can be used in both negative and positive situations:
- Negative: mapping the impact of a dysfunctional boss
- Positive: mapping the investment impact of leadership development

Premise: Every human reaction whether in attitude or behavior has a ripple effect.

Ripple Effect *defined*:
a *spreading effect* or *series of consequences* caused by a single action

Here's my observation and belief => if decision-makers could see and quantify the *full impact* (or ripple effect) of performance, they would spend money on the people side of the business differently. And that's why the practice of creating impact maps to diagnose and assess is tremendously valuable. It's an invaluable tool in developing behavior literacy!

Additional Ripple Effect Considerations
(both in tangible and intangible categories)

In the spirit of seeing the big picture, to follow are common elements to contemplate that may need to appear on your impact map. The goal is to create a comprehensive map. The items below are not intended to be all inclusive, certainly there'll be other industry or company specific elements to include.

Financial

> Increase in revenue
> Cost reduction
> Sustained revenue
> Sales numbers

Customer
> Retention = sustained profits
> Additional customer acquisition
> Release unprofitable customers

Productivity
> Timely achievement of goals & objectives
> Motivation, engagement (saves on turnover costs)
> Targeted value activity

Employees
> Retention (saves on turnover costs)
> Work satisfaction & morale for self and others
> Improved performance reviews
> Promotion, succession, talent retention
> Letting go of toxic employees and/or managers

Well-being (saves on missed days, productivity, team morale)
Family support
Savings on health benefits
Fewer E.A.P. visits; absenteeism
Reducing stress

Innovation - Creativity - Idea generation
New products, profitable tweaks to existing products / services

Personal (motivation)

Improved Communication
Productivity
Motivation
Increased speed to results
Minimize or avoid mistakes

Effective decision-making
Productivity
Better results

Learning (knowledge value)
Minimizing counterproductive/sabotaging behavior
Engagement impact

In Summary

... questions, ratings and mapping are simple, yet highly effective tools in assessing the effect of situations, incidents, return-on-investment or even employee value-added contributions. Ultimately, you have to see the big picture to make the best decisions.

These activities help in seeing beyond the person, learning to look at behavior and its results, and surveying the impact both short and long term. It's learning to competently work with intangibles.

"Leadership should be born out of the understanding of the needs of those who would be affected by it."
- Marian Anderson

WORKSHEET

The previous ROI list is a great place to source when creating your impact map. Additionally, provided below is a general calculation worksheet and is specifically related to mapping and measuring the cost of turnover.

Summary Worksheet: Measuring the Cost of Turnover

Whenever calculating cost related to turnover, there are common elements to include. Here is a generic list. I recommend you create a customized template specifically for your company.

Considerations:
Cost of Turnover = Separation Costs + Replacement Costs + Orientation-Training/Costs + ramp up time to optimal performance

Separation Costs:
1. Separation Pay: $?
2. Continued benefits contribution?
3. Unemployment tax

Replacement Costs:
4. Communication of Vacancy - ads, electronic recruiting & posting,
5. Recruiting - staffing firm engagement
6. Pre-employment admin
7. Selection interviews (time spent = $ hourly value of hiring manager or HR professional)
8. (If hiring manager: time / cost = spent away from other productivity/key activities.)
   Exception: It's not a cost if company has an integrated talent management process, where talent acquisition is considered a regular part of the manager's job description and company practices = recruiting not a one-time event in crisis, but an ongoing activity of looking for good people.
9. Testing – Fit for Duty Assessments (drug testing, background checks, best fit assessments)
10. Relocation Expense

Orientation / Training
1. Materials – books, e-learning courses
2. Equipment - boots, uniform, technology
3. Formal training
4. Training wages
5. OJT observation (ojt = on the job training)
6. Estimated ramp-up period to maximum productivity? *(generic estimate from the Future Foundation Study 6-8 months, then determine*

incremental % of compensation #s to scale (you're determining roi as mentioned earlier, over the ramp up period).

Turnover Summary Totals
Cost of Turnover – Total from each category
1. Separation Costs
2. Replacement Costs
3. Training Costs
4. Ramp up to needed performance

Yearly Overall Cost of Turnover Summary *(if this applies to you)*
Estimated cost in your workforce annually (use your employee count and turnover #):
Turnover Rate X Turnover Cost = Total Annual Cost

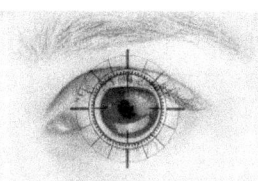

Fine Tune Your Eye – Increase Your Sensitivity

Let's look at a few more examples.

To follow are 3 situations that can be found in any organization. *As you read through the examples…*
- try to identify key behaviors
- consider the operational impact (take a shot at determining the ripple effect via an impact map)
- try calculating or estimating potential financial costs
- think about what behaviors could have been in place to mitigate the adverse outcomes or contributed to a constructive, positive outcome. Adding this piece creates the framework for a development plan that could be used to coach the gap.

> By the way, this is a great exercise to do with your leadership team and HR department.
> We use this exercise, among others, in our leadership development roundtables.

EXAMPLES

#1   The Gruff & Rough HR Manager

Linda is the key HR point-of-contact for all employees in a 125-person company. She is known to be efficient in executing all employee paperwork and keeping employee records in impeccable shape.

Unfortunately, she is also known to be impatient and insensitive in her relating style when employees come to the human resources department for help with issues concerning co-workers and direct reports.

Recently, an employee had a legitimate concern about being sexually harassed by her manager. It had gotten to the point where she was feeling very embarrassed and equally fearful of losing her job. The mounting pressure and anxiety she was experiencing was generating severe headaches resulting in sick days. Clearly it was getting to the point where she needed to reveal what was happening and get help. Yet, she kept putting it off.

Why? She knew that the person she would need to reveal this to was none other than the HR Manager who had a reputation for a lack of empathy and tact. This reputation fueled the harassed employee's fear of bringing this critical situation to the appropriate people, compounding her stress and anxiety.

In the end, the employee left and sued the company for sexual harassment, resulting in her winning a significant financial settlement, and the firing of the harassing manager.

Assessment

Let's look at the HR Manager scenario. Here are some questions and as you answer, these, chart out an impact map (feel free to reference the Ripple Effect list). Remember – everything has a ripple effect. To where and what extent needs to be carefully considered.

- What behaviors on the part of the HR Manager contributed to this financial loss?
- What behaviors on the part of the harassing manager were involved?

- Who else could the manager been harassing and what kind of liability exposure has gone unreported?
- Where were the areas of financial loss in this story beyond the obvious of the settlement (e.g. sick days, lower productivity of the employee…etc.)?
- What would be the competencies needed (or "critical success factors") for an HR Manager to be effective?
- How would those competencies positively contribute to a company's bottom line?

Conclusion: The absence of needed relational skills and other behaviors had a meaningful impact on the company's bottom line. The irony? A minimal investment in management or executive coaching could have helped this key employee develop the sensitivity and relational skills needed to appropriately and adequately handle this legally volatile situation.

Additionally, had the HR Manager been more competent, she could have set up a coaching arrangement for the harassing manager and perhaps could have turned around the situation and appropriately coached the inappropriate, illegal behavior.

These are situations where, as a solution provider, I periodically meet resistance to invest in coaching. It's clear that intervention of some kind is needed. Here's the truth – **you will pay a little now or inevitably pay a lot later.**

#2   Entry Level Sales Employees

A promising, newly hired employee with a "go-getter" personality has been hired with high hopes of significantly increasing revenue and new customers.

Initially, this employee with a very outgoing personality was performing well and well on his way to great success. However, as the next few months unfolded, his sales numbers started to decline.

His manager, who had been a successful self-starter and break out star with a similar personality, could not understand what was going on. He'd had little management training and therefore no practical knowledge or resources to help his potential star work through the slow down. This left the situation floundering for both the manager and the new sales employee for the next several quarters.

Eventually, the sales manager became frustrated and found it hard to constructively manage. His frustration came from two key places; the loss of sales revenue and his own sense of inadequacy in helping this young "go-getter" regain his positive performance.

The increasing frustration began to erode the rapport between the manager and sales member and the rising star was transferred to a different role, which was not aligned with his potential. Eventually, he left the organization altogether.

The interesting part of this story is that the sales star ended up at another organization which happened to have an exemplary sales and management training program. He found his footing and became a consistently high performer.

Had the manager learned to competently coach this high potential, he would have learned that beliefs impact behavior which produces results. What came to light in subsequent sales training with the new company is he felt like asking for the sale in the style he was trained seemed too "pushy". If the manager had helped him reframe his beliefs and develop a more comfortable closing style, he could have begun to close sales again – all without leaving his position.

Assessment
Questions:
- How could this have been handled differently?
- How could the manager have been coached to not loose this talented employee?
- How is this manager's inability to effectively coach impacting the profitability with other members of the sales team?
- What's the ripple effect of this management skill deficit to company revenue?
- What other questions would be important to ask?
- What conclusions can you draw?

Tip: *Your ripple effect impact map*
can also assist in crafting additional questions.

#3 Summary Example - Disrespectful, Abusive Boss

One behavior… a chain reaction
This example is quick, easy and unfortunately all too common.

A lead supervisor is disrespectful to everyone on her team and abusive in the way she treats them.

Every time she has direct interaction with any member of her team it translates into that member being demotivated. Not only is the motivation of the employee diminished, so is the focus.

In this situation, it's common for employees to become distracted by discussing and complaining with fellow employees, which takes up work time, focus, and energy that could be spent getting accomplishing meaningful work.

It's clear that disrespectful, abusive behavior directly impacts the productivity of employees and creates a ripple effect to the customers and ultimately the bottom line.

Additionally, talented self-confident employees tend to have a low tolerance for this kind of behavior and their tenure will be short knowing they can be employed elsewhere in a better environment. (At the end of this briefing is a worksheet template for calculating turnover.)

Additional costs to consider:
- Stress related absences
- Cost to conduct a search for those who have left
- Ramp up time for new employee to reach full productivity

Perhaps you are getting more adept at reading and assessing behavior. The ability to answer the questions provided (in addition to adding your own) by key leadership and those actively engaged in talent management is critical to the connection between behavior and profits.

This activity is an essential prelude to strategic planning for training and development and/or coaching vs. uninformed and/or random training. It's also the prelude to how you will decide to spend money on any activity that serves the human side of the enterprise. And finally, it creates the context for how you will assess return-on-investment.

Related to example #3, I must share a real ripple effect story.

The scene: A manufacturing facility making a common product — potato chips that has an oppressive, uninformed management.

The situation: A public relations nightmare.

This potato chip facility, with a headcount of 210 employees, had fired 58 in the first nine months of 1973 for disciplinary reasons. Morale was poisonous. Managers in the plant were frustrated, because, in spite of ceaseless disciplinary actions — written warnings, disciplinary suspensions without pay, terminations — employee misbehavior continued unabated. Workers in the plant, angry and resentful about the constant warnings and reprimands and discharges, sought any available means to strike back.

One ingenious worker discovered a cunning way to communicate his unhappiness with the way the plant's brass was running the place. He came to work one day armed with a felt-tipped pen.

He had discovered that it was possible to surreptitiously remove a potato chip from the conveyor belt that ran between the production and packaging areas, write a vulgar message on it, and replace it undetected. The vandalized potato chip would not be discovered until it was literally in the consumer's hands.

Word spread quickly among the employees about his unique trick for getting even with management for their harsh treatment of the hourly staff. Other workers joined in. Consumer complaints grew. Every day at the potato chip maker's corporate headquarters the mail brought angrier letters from customers, outraged at finding indecent love letters written on the potato chips they had bought.

What was causing all of the problems in this plant? On the surface, this plant seemed no different from any of the other 38 facilities that were operated around the country, making snack foods out of potatoes and corn. But at this plant the discipline system had simply run amok. As employee problems increased, supervisors took more disciplinary action. Harsher supervisory behavior led to increased employee mischief and misbehavior. Instead of producing solved problems and improved performance, more discipline simply generated more violations. The discipline system, intended to correct employee misbehavior, was in fact encouraging it. The traditional discipline system had failed.

Source: Dick Grote - Discipline Without Punishment

I'm sure you get the point, *but just in case…*

Here are additional examples of behaviors that directly impact a company's bottom line. Some of these listed are subtle, but when you really consider the ripple effect, it's eye-opening:

- Dominating relating style of a manager– not giving others a chance to contribute…I call that "leaving talent on the table"
- Resistance or refusal to learn something new and useful
- Blocked access to talent - employee difficult to approach due to abrasive and combative interpersonal style
- Adversely impact collaboration due to same behaviors
- A manager that has a hard time saying no to interruptions and there is reduced productivity due to focus disruption.
- Worker absenteeism due to difficult, disruptive co-workers gone unaddressed

Though the scenarios shared were leader based, the same holds true for individual contributors. The point -- behaviors from any employee either constructively contribute to the greater good or they don't.

We must become more sensitive and responsive to behaviors that are not supporting the outcomes that the majority of your leaders and employees are working so hard to achieve.

Solution #2: Learn to Measure, Quantify, & Valuate Behavior ...and its impact

Here's where everything starts to go south. I was having a conversation with a president and we were discussing the unfortunate performance of one of his key leaders.

Identifying the behaviors seemed easy enough. Then I asked this question, *"How much do you think this is costing you?"* His response and facial expression was common – akin to the "dear in the headlight" look – his mouth shaped with an inaudible, "What?"

When working with decision-makers, we talk a lot about how to apply value, measure performance and use metrics. It creates a ball of confusion they are desperate to solve. We explore questions such as:
- ⇨ How do we measure behavior?
- ⇨ How do we quantitate the intangibles?
- ⇨ What do we want to measure?
- ⇨ How do we measure value?
- ⇨ What additional metrics do we want to use?
- ⇨ And ultimately, how do we determine return-on-investment

All of these can be done with one or all of what I call "the key three":

- ✓ Numbers #
- ✓ Percentages %
- ✓ Dollars $

Many times, to calculate financial impact (moving intangibles to tangibles), the process of measuring comes in that order –> numbers that can be turned into percentages and translated into dollars.

We help our clients generate data from the intangibles and that's how we as growth partners determine our contribution. Every leader, manager, and business owner needs to know how to do this. **They need to know their unique financial impact.**

So how do you measure behavior?

Well, here's the good news, you already are in 2 fundamental ways -- through wages and performance feedback!

Once you've determined a salary or hourly wage for an employee, you've decided to measure the value and contribution of that employee to your company revenue in the context of time. This becomes the base from which most other measurements can occur.

Simple ROI – we expect this (job description) to occur for the agreed upon amount of money

With that expectation in mind, the 2nd common ROI practice is assessing performance by way of an appraisal or review. This process determines if expectations have been met by answering the question, "Am I getting what I'm paying for? Is performance less than, equal to or more than what's expected via the job description?" For those who have a more formal performance management, ratings (#s) are assigned.

These are 2 examples of **base ROI** which we call **return-on-compensation,** reflected in dollars and numbers. We'll expand on this in an upcoming segment.

First, we're going to look at several examples of measure, quantifying, and valuating behavior from a macro perspective.

Part A: Can Behavior Be Measured? - Macro Example #1
The Future Foundation Study

Several years ago a study was conducted by The Future Foundation, the result of which was entitled *The Cost of Poor People Management*. 700 executives across the globe were surveyed. It included the countries of the United Kingdom, Sweden, the Netherlands, the United States, Hong Kong, India and Australia. Their polling put forth a series of fundamental questions about the philosophy of – and approaches to – people management.

Here are some findings related to the United States:

"Organizations in the U.S. are failing to actualize the latent human potential within their workforces and to address the performance issues hindering sustainable success. Indeed, poor people management is one of the worst hidden costs facing U.S. companies.

Overall, the U.S. is devoting $105 billion a year to correcting problems associated with poor hiring and people management practices. This shortfall is worth 1.05% of the total U.S. GDP. The reason for this loss of capital in the U.S., as uncovered in The Future Foundation study, is that businesses waste the talent and potential of their workforces and fail to match the right people to the right jobs.

The research reveals that an average of <u>eight months is necessary to attain required on-the-job performance levels</u>, which makes mismatches between person and job prove costly for both employees and their companies. Employees themselves are neither blind nor impervious to the demoralizing effects of poor people management practices. In fact, nearly a quarter (23%) of U.S. workers surveyed believe their colleagues are incompetent.

U.S. managers waste an average of 34 days per year dealing with underperformance. Senior executives claim they spend seven weeks a year -- or over an hour per day -- managing badly performing employees.

More worrying still, U.S. employees admit that 68% of the mistakes they personally make never come to their managers' attention.

By not matching the right people with the right jobs, U.S. companies are also compromising the productivity of their experienced, well-paid managers, because their managerial time could be more productively spent on value-adding tasks. And the problems increase with organizational size. U.S. managers in larger organizations (>$8.5M in turnover) are spending 41 days, or eight weeks per year, on managing poor performers."

Source link: http://www.inc.com/articles/2004/12/karsh.html

I encourage you to read the entire article and report. It addresses many of the messages expressed in this briefing.

Though we're not privy to the all the numbers collected, the results of this report are an example of numbers turned into percentages, numbers extracted from an intangible – hiring practices and the ripple effect related to use of time and productivity.

Though hiring is a physical, tangible act, contained in that act are plenty of intangibles such as knowledge, decision-making, and unconscious bias to name a few.

These human elements produce results that can be translated into numbers, dollars and percentages. This capability (and I know I sound like a broken record) needs to be part of every business plan and strategy.

Example: Unconscious bias can undermine hiring diverse candidates. This can be detected with tangible numbers from workforce hiring.

"If you think hiring professionals is expensive, try hiring amateurs."
-Anonymous

Macro Example #2: Company Stock Price When Investing in Talent Development

Laurie Bassi is the chairwoman and Daniel McMurrer is the chief research officer of Knowledge Asset Management, a money management firm in Bethesda, Maryland. Here is a commentary on the theme of stock price impact when a company consistently invests in talent development

Title: Employees cost or profit source...invest in their development and see the results

"Managers are always claiming, "People are our most important asset." But deep down, they can't shake the feeling that employees are costs. Big costs. And they treat them that way. Quarterly earnings off? Cut the perks, rein in training, and downsize. This strategy may increase earnings in the short term, but it's myopic. Recent studies suggest that layoffs actually destroy shareholder value. And our research shows that treating employees like the assets they are—by investing in their development—boosts returns over the long term.

For years now, our research has measured the effect of spending on employee education and training—a "cost" that is buried in general and administrative expenses—on the stock prices of 575 publicly traded firms. We created four hypothetical portfolios (one each for years 1997 through 2000) consisting of between 20 and 40 companies that invested at roughly twice the industry norm in employee development in each of the previous years (1996 through 1999). We followed the performance of these portfolios through 2001. Their returns were robust and in line with a growing body of empirical research showing that organizations that make extraordinary investments in people often enjoy extraordinary performance on a variety of indicators, including shareholder return.

In December 2001, we decided to put our money where our research was and created a live portfolio of companies that spend aggressively on employee development. In its first 25 months since inception, that portfolio has outperformed the S&P 500 index by 4.6 percentage points (2.2% versus a decline of 2.4% for the index). In January 2003, we expanded our investment strategy by launching two additional live equity portfolios made up of similar development-oriented companies.

The results speak for themselves. While past performance is never a guarantee of future results, and while it is always possible to lose money, each of these three portfolios outperformed the S&P 500 by 17% to 35% in 2003."

Source: Harvard Business Review Online - 2004 | by Laurie Bassi and Daniel McMurrer
http://support.aspentech.com/supportpublictrain/HowIsYourReturnOnPeople.pdf

Part B: Measuring Behavior in Standard Business Operations
Calculating costs associated with employee performance

As I mentioned at the start, one of the most important competencies any "talent management practitioner" / human resource manager which again is any business leader, those with P&L responsibility, HR professional or those who lead people in any capacity, could have is the ability to calculate costs associated with employee performance (return-on-compensation) as well as their own. Very few know how or a willing to do learn (I think it's a fundamental aversion to math -- I can totally relate!)

This solution will help you and your staff create a foundation from which to work. We'll use a few popular scenarios and related costs. You'll discover as you continue, that there are some consistent themes or costs in just about every scenario and therefore, most cost areas used in the calculations are pretty standard.

Again, in every scenario the ripple effect needs to be considered. Don't forget the *chain reaction, so constructing your impact map* will provide a more comprehensive picture.

As you review the following examples (numbers are applied where available and applicable), begin to craft you own templates and customize them.

Expanding On Baseline ROI

As mentioned earlier, unrecognized by many leaders is the fact that return on investment, is automatically built into standard business operation. The moment you write a job description and determine an hourly wage or salary, you set the stage to determine ROI. You've established spend (an investment amount) towards operational activities for

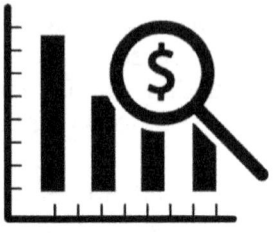

which you're needing a return aka results. You are turning an intangible into a tangible.

Additionally, once that arrangement is made, that person (no matter what you call them – employee, team member, associate -- or whatever title you give them – director, manager, or supervisor) **becomes a business partner**. Employing someone reflects shared expectations and agreements in contributing to the success of the business.

This arrangement sets the framework for a business' base return-on-investment involving 2 constants in measuring any performance ROI – compensation and time applied to job activities.

As the decision-maker, you are thinking…

1. **Compensation => How much am I spending to achieve specific outcomes?** …that is achieving desired performance or results (meeting expectations / performance for an agreed $ amount).

    You can assess performance easily with 3 simple criteria - performance below expectations – at expectations – or above (adding value).

    The answer to this question will help you determine your "return on investment" for the salary or hourly amount spent. Are you getting what you paid for?

If the performance is below, **its now becoming a cost/expense – you are losing money.** If this is true, additional considerations would be wise. Ask, "How is this impacting the rest of the team and/or other stakeholders?"…other departments, customer/clients as an example. In other words, "How much is this costing us in other areas?"

This is particularly important to identify if it's a manager. If an underperforming or dysfunctional manager is the issue, the ripple effect of cost could be significant. If the manager is underperforming, it's more than likely he/she is causing others to do the same. **Now your loss is multiplying until a change is made.**

This is a great example of adverse and significant P/L impact and something that requires keen attention because it's not reflected in day to day traditional accounting activity, but will show up in a variety of ways over time.

> This example also makes a case for something we discussed earlier – the need to determine and closely track **KPIs – key people indicators**. Imagine how much money would be saved if the impact of a bad manager was caught early!

2. **Time => In what time framework do I want needed outcomes to be achieved?**

Time, like money, is a basic, fixed resource for any function in business. So if you are new to identifying key metrics, time can always be used first. Time along with money (compensation) can be included in every impact issue you encounter.

Key to using time, is determining what's an acceptable amount of time to execute needed outcomes – what might be called usual or customary. This can be a bit challenging to determine for roles or functions where "usual or customary" time usage has never been determined.

75

In many white collar jobs, as an example, it's not common to know specific time usage or how long certain functions take. I've said in many time management workshops, "When managers set expectations for deliverables, in many cases they have no idea how long certain activities will take." No benchmarking has occurred and performance expectations are based on a miscellaneous feel or perception.

In our time management workshop, we talk about the use of time mapping to determine reasonable timeframes for setting expectations, educating the employee and the manager.

So let's work through some typical workplace scenarios to practice measuring, quantifying and valuating behavior.

=> **Recommend Action:** As your read through the various examples to follow, plug in your numbers to get a feel for the act of calculating. Start practicing now. Also, I give detailed calculations. I know there are a variety of math routes to get to the same summary numbers.

Example & Exercise #1 –
Measuring Behavior & Its Financial Impact

Scenario: **Severely underperforming supervisor/manager**

Impact => productivity, compensation
ROI, ripple effect

Situation: Everything on the resume looked like an excellent fit. Yet, once the person was hired, all sorts of odd behaviors began to surface along with an alarming level of inability to make decisions, lead the team and adequately fill the role. It was a huge distraction and time sucker for the direct report.

Management Decision: Kept on board, did not let go for a duration of one year. (This was a real situation from a manager I know. I asked her recently, "In retrospect, what would you have done differently?" She answered, "Followed my gut, not tried to make excuses to explain the odd behavior and complete disconnect from the resume to reality and let her go. I just kept thinking, a warm body is better than no body. I've determined that was not true.")

Determining the true time lost in this situation was enormous, but was estimated to be at least 1-2 hours a day, which trickled into weekends for the Direct Report due to productivity losses.

Preliminary Cost

What to consider (remember items from the impact map section):
- o Loss productivity of direct report
- o Loss roi of compensation for underperforming manager
- o Ripple effect impact to team
- o Impact to customers
- o What else would you add? (see ripple effect list)

a. **Time / productivity of direct report** – when calculating using an hourly wage number is the easiest place to begin. $60,000 annual salary / 40 hrs wk/ 50 wks a year (2 wks vacation)

$60,000 divided by 2,000 hrs of workable time = $30.00 /hr

Let's use 2 hours of loss productivity of direct report primarily used coaching and addressing underperformance = 10 hours a week

10 x $30/hour = $300.00 week x 4 weeks = $1,200/month x 12 = $14,400 year => Direct report lost compensation value (based on scenario this is incredibly low)

b. **Lack of productivity of supervisor and fulfillment of performance expectation** - *Take hourly rate x hours lost*

Annual salary: $40,000 / approximately $21.00/hr
We'll use 2 hours (which is conservative knowing the situation)
2 hrs x $21.00 = $42.00 x 5 days = $210.00 wk x 4 wks = $840.00 /mth x 12 = $10,080.00 year

Total so far: $24,480.00 (manager & direct report)

> Now let's calculate the ripple effect cost <

c. Impacted team member(s) - @ $30,000 yearly salary
Determine impact time/hr follow the same as above - an hour

We'll use 3 team members with loss productivity (or needed job performance) of 1 hour a day at the same hourly rate = (3 x $16)

Let's do the numbers first via # of hours:
3 hours a day loss productivity | 3 hours x $16/hr = $48.00/day
Hours lost = 3 x 5= 15/wk x 4 = 60/ mth x 12 = 720 loss for the year, which is actually **90 days of lost productivity** *– 720 hours / 8 a day = 90*

Stop and think about this –
90 days is 3 months of lost productivity! That's a wow!

Now, let's do the dollars:
$48.00 x 5 days in a week = $240.00 x 4wks = $960.00 x 12 months = $11,520 cost per year.

Estimated total loss of return-on-compensation from 1 underperforming supervisor based on decision to retain for one year:

Direct Report / Manager = $14,400.00
The Supervisor = $10,800.00
The team = $11,520.00
Total cost over the year: $36,720.00

I'm confident, due to the intimate knowledge of the situation, this figure is significantly low. Also, considering the ripple effect, I'm confident there was an adverse impact to customers resulting in reduced sales, lost sales and retention. Those numbers were not available.

Knowing the business, I can safely say this one scenario's financial impact, on the conservative side, was easily in the range of a $40-$50,000 loss – on the high side perhaps $50-$75,000.

In fact, consider the high side – it's is more than the entire salary of the direct report, but for sure the entire salary of the supervisor. **It actually cost money to keep the underperforming supervisor.**

Think about it…
It's like paying someone to help you loose money.

Hum…

Interesting thought: I always think it's interesting when an ineffective or dysfunctional manager asks for a raise while they are costing their company money. This is a true sign of not being behavior or financially literate.

What would happen if they were presented with their unique *"leadership balance sheet"*? For an example, in calculating cost of turnover for a bully boss where 3 of 5 team members quit including the ripple effect, I wonder what those numbers would be in comparison to his/her compensation?

A Broader View – Determine What's at Risk & Long Term Impact
Numbers Paint a Picture

In each of the examples used so far, we've looked at what we consider low impact scenarios. It would also be useful to look at a broader impact, view, and approach.

When considering either positive or negative impact, in leadership for example, to a department or business unit, you can first determine what's financially at stake. To do so, **start with the total compensation of a group.** That number is the initial financial exposure that could increase or decrease depending on group performance and leadership impact.

This view is especially important because it can capture the broadest assessment of the ripple effect. Let's use the earlier scenario regarding productivity, but with a higher level leader - VP of Sales.

Scenario: Major distractions due to dysfunctional leadership.

We'll use productivity as the base, but in doing a ripple effect impact map, you would certainly include sales numbers, as well as customer/client retention among other elements. So the number to follow reflects potentially a *small percentage* of impact.

Compensation Numbers:
VP base $155,000
Division has 5 Regional Directors – each with a team of 6
Regional Directors' base compensation - $95,000 x 5 = $475,000
Base compensation for 30 team members - $65,000 = **$1,950,000***
Total base compensation for this division = $4,530,000**

*Think about this. When hiring a leader of a large group, look at the amount of money that will be impacted by the competency or lack there of that leader.

***This is the amount at risk if performance is below what's expected*

The behavior of the VP is creating a disruptive, distracting division culture that has trickled down to each region and team member, resulting in lack of focus and loss productivity within the division.

To calculate impact, we'll use a minimum of 1 hour a day of lost productivity for all members This equals 250 hours per person for the year if no intervention occurs.

Here's the numbers (based on 40 hrs / 50 wks – 2,000 /hrs – expected work hours)

VP - $77.50 /hr | Regional Dir. - $74.50/hr | Team member - $32.50/hr

Dollar Loss / Reduced Return-on-Compensation (annualized)
VP - $19,375.00
Directors - $18,625 x 5 = $93,125.00
Team member - $8,125.00 x 30 = $243,750.00

Total minimum loss for the division: $356,250.00 *without any additional items from the ripple effect impact map. This represents 7.86% loss of total compensation for the division.*

Recommended exercise for your company => Determine the total compensation invested for each team or department (this can be eye-opening). Now examine who is leading each team or department and how they are impacting the investment – maintaining, increasing (adding value) or loosing?

Additionally, when numbers are seen from this point of view, the concept of needing management /leadership training or executive coaching should no longer be an issue! In most cases, we've seen that the investment is no comparison to the dollars loss or potential gain.

Get the Big Picture – Is There a Long Term Impact?
Here's one last element to include. The calculations represented above are in the context of a year, starting with weekly numbers. In assessing a situation, factor in:
- how long the situation has existed and
- what, if any, long term financial impact there may be.

This piece really matters!

Solution #3: See the Use of Money Differently

 If leaders want to continue to meet the ever changing needs of acquiring and managing their talent in a way that supports their company growth, they must see the use of money differently. Perhaps the previous examples have helped.

Many leaders are stifling or even suffocating their growth because they see their finances and money in very black and white terms – for example "have it or not", "in the budget or not", rather than seeing it as a strategic resource to invest vs. a cost.

Everything discussed in this briefing so far influences a key decision-marker's approach to enhancing the very business elements that are under greater scrutiny by investors and identified as intangibles.

For example, it's very common to have significant hesitation in spending money on what we commonly know as employee training and development, including management and leadership training.

And it makes perfect sense when considering the definition of investing:
⇒ To put money to use
⇒ To put money into something offering potential profitable returns and value

> *If, in fact, a decision-maker does not see or believe there will be a meaningful return, they will see it as a cost rather than an investment.* The psychological aspect of cost feels like a loss, it's as if something is being taken away—even the feeling of waste. There is no sense of gain. Certainly it would even feel irresponsible to spend the money.

I truly believe many decision-makers feel this way. If they do decide to spend money, it's as if they are taking a bitter pill. It may seem logical and necessary, but think, "I'm not going to like it and let's not go overboard and spend too much."

That's why this section and briefing in general is so important. As we've discussed, this common occurrence is not serving companies well.

By the way, for some leaders, meaningful return is not measured in money, but in meeting a personal value or emotional need. One client recently said, "I'm really not so much concerned about the money. I just know they need help and if they feel they're being supported, that's what matters most to me." This sentiment harkens back to the piece, *Leaders Have Feelings Too*. It's an intangible need being met.

Measuring ROI Example #2 – A Time Management Workshop

Let's look at another common example of money spent and sometimes seen as a cost – an employee training/development workshop-seminar. This is a great example of using our 2 basic ROI criteria - time & money and also serves as an example of profitable/unprofitable behavior -- how behavior impacts ROI and "ROC" (return-on-compensation).

One of the most popular workshops I've taught across the country is Organizational Strategies for the Overwhelmed (I love that title!).

When I begin the workshop, I usually go through a discussion of what the participants most want to get out of the day. One of the most common needs is dealing with unwanted interruptions from co-workers.

Though there are many ways to approach it, I give a four-step process that is tactful, respectful and easy to implement.

As I reveal the 4 steps, I ask them to calculate how much time would be saved (or as I say recaptured for reallocation) if the tip were implemented.

Reminder: 2 base measuring factors for almost any employee performance are compensation and time. Measuring and determining ROI is looking for and translating performance into #s, %, and $.

The attendees are amazed how much time is impacted and can be recaptured when they do the calculation for implementing just one tip, beginning with a day, then translating those numbers into a year.

One participant indicated he would not only recapture time for himself, but also help other team members as well (the ripple effect). But for the sake of the exercise, we just worked his numbers.

Here's his numbers:

Time Saved:
He indicated he would save on average 1 hour a day x 5 days in his work week = 5 hours a week x 4 weeks = 20 hours (that's 2.5 days for the month).

If the tip was consistently implemented over a period of time...
Over the course of one quarter = 20 hours a month x 3 months = 60 hours; 60 hours in a quarter x 4 quarters in a year = 240 hours

How many days is that?...assuming 8 hours day = 240 hours /8 = 30 days recaptured... that's one work month and a week (25 work days) just from implementing that one tip!

Money Saved:
Now let's convert time saved into money. Let's say he is a salaried management employee who earns $55,000 a year. Let's break down the numbers:

In this case, we're going to turn the yearly salary into an hourly number: (forward slash represents divided by)

$55,000 / 12 = $4,583.00 - month / 4 weeks = $ 1,145.75 / 5 days = $229.15 / 8 hours
= $22.44 /hour

Hours recaptured 240 hours x $22.44 = $5,385.60

Reminder: Whenever behavior change is being measured, the ripple effect should be considered. We could then ask, "How has this manager's behavior change impacted members of his team?"

In the case of time management, it is very reasonable to think that the ripple effect could reasonably be ½ hour a day for each team member (and that's without them attending the workshop). Consider the additional impact if an entire team attended and successfully implemented only one tip!

With that assumption and for the sake of this exercise, let's continue the ROI calculation. Let's say this manager has 5 employees, each at about $35,000 in salary. Let's work the numbers.

Time Saved:
5 employee x ½ hour a day = 2.5 hours x 5 days = 12.5 x 4 weeks = 50 hours in a month x 3 months (1 quarter) – 150 hours x 4 months = 600 hours for the year.

Money Saved:
Assuming an 8 hour day = 1920 hours in a year / $35,000 = $18.23 / hour for each team member

600 hours x $18.23 = $10,938 combined with the manager's savings, that totals: $16,323.60 - saved on 1 tip with a modest ripple effect.

If each team member achieved the same savings of 1 hour a day – that would be $21,876.00 + the manager's that would be $27,261.60

> *Thought:* Consider the scale of the VP of Sales scenario numbers. If the entire division had time management/productivity training-coaching, the loss numbers could have been in the plus column. That could be an roi of $356,250 from 1 training/development initiative and probably a positive impact on sales. The return-on-investment could be amazing!

Final ROI

Let's say the average cost of a time management workshop is in the range of $3,000-$5,000. Subtract the cost ($3,000) from the total savings and the final ROI number would be $24,261.60.

Earlier I mentioned ROI can be calculated in #, %, and/or $. We have the number and the dollars. To calculate %, here is the basic formula:

$$\frac{\text{Results} - \text{Cost}}{\text{Cost}} \times 100\% = \text{ROI}$$

So using the 1 hour per week for each team member and manager number of $27,161.60, it would look like this:

$$\frac{\$27,161.60 - \$3,000 \ (\$24,261.60)}{\$3,000} \quad X = \text{return on investment} - 808\%$$

Important conclusions from this example...

In this example, when a decision-maker says they cannot afford this type of workshop, it's technically not true. The money is there and being applied to labor at a certain level of return-on-compensation. An investment in this type of workshop could substantially improve that in addition to creating a profitable ripple effect.

Technically, from a strategic perspective, the money needs to be invested to improve productivity so that a better return on compensation can be achieved -- it's a wise use of operating funds.

Operational Insights
✓ Low productivity / performance = Low compensation ROI
✓ Sometimes you have to spend money to save more money
✓ With a demonstrated ROI, spending money is really just using money to generate more money
✓ Spend is only a cost if it's subtracting from the P/L rather than adding to it

There is also a broader lesson here. Most employee training and development activities are seen as a stand alone event. Yet if used strategically, it's really an *operational performance decision*.

Let's say for example a leader wants to grow the company. Logically, growth will need to be handled by the employees. That means they will need to increase their performance capacity.

One way to achieve that is to help them increase productivity so that they can "make room for more". A simple time management workshop or productivity coach could accomplish this. So the the cost of the workshop, now becomes a *strategic investment* vs. a stand alone cost.

When considering the spend, *first look at the results* <u>*you want*</u> to achieve. Make a list. Let's do this with the above scenario:
- ✓ Increase capacity
- ✓ Increased confidence
- ✓ Ability to mange overwhelm
- ✓ Increased team collaboration
- ✓ Increased productivity which immediately translates into increased return-on-compensation.
- ✓ Investing in the intangibles to get more tangibles

I'm sure you can identify more. Now, in looking at this list and thinking of your team, if these outcomes were achieved, applying a dollar amount, how much would it be worth to you? I'm guessing whatever number you decide, it's probably substantially more than the average cost of the workshop or coach.

|> Leadership Insight
When considering spend, many decision-makers are not clear on their desired outcomes. Or, if they do have a sense of what they want to achieve, they tend to focus more on the money being spent rather than the value and benefits of the outcomes they'll obtain.

Other Scenarios – ROI Impact

To follow is a list of results commonly known as 'soft skills'. Taking any of the items below, a ripple effect-impact map could be created that could translate into dollars, ultimately impacting revenue. So yes, as we've learned throughout this briefing, soft skills can be measured.

Some are a simple connection to dollars (#1), others will require a few additional elements (#5).

ROI examples from training and/or coaching that can be translated into $, %, #s (these are also great scenarios in learning to read behavior).

1. Star Salesperson increases revenue with 1 quarter of coaching

2. Executive improves communication to key team members *result* increased levels of trust = a costly mistake is caught earlier

3. Executive improves communication *result* valued leader decides to stay (no turnover costs)

4. Key leader improves his/her decision-making *result* action is taken quicker, team members have more trust in their leadership, productivity increases for everyone.

5. Key leader more assertive *result* team members gain confidence in leader, become more responsive productivity increases, key financial metrics increase.

6. High potential is more engaged due to resolved hurts – begins problem solving key issues – presented an implemental idea resulting in savings on process.

7. Team is more organized due to better leadership *result* getting more done and proactively assessing needs

8. Leader begins to demonstrate more caring & respect for team – they become more responsive (spend less time grumbling & complaining) focus & productivity increase.

A great assessment mantra = **Map it, then Measure it!**

A Simple Story of ROI

Several months ago I had a supervisor in a coaching group who had a less than positive attitude towards one of his new employees. In fact, he'd labeled the employee "lazy" – though he'd not taken the time to get to know him.

In accepting the challenge from the coaching group to build positive rapport with each team member to improve motivation, he made it a goal to talk with and get to know this new member. In the process of doing so, the supervisor asked him if he liked his job. To his surprise, the team member said yes and mentioned no one had ever asked him if he did or if he wanted to do more. The supervisor then asked if he'd be willing to help him with a special project to which the team member happily agreed. He was asked to do a follow up count of product being shipped and in doing so caught 4 counting mistakes that translated into a savings that week of appx. $2,000.

Subsequently at the next group coaching meeting, the supervisor was happy to report the results and what he'd learned, and all participants were able to hear and be motivated by the continuing ripple effect week to week from that experience.

This story, of many I experience, is a tangible map to ROI from coaching with accountability. **When you activate behavior change, you will get measurable results.**

"Investing is the intersection of economics and psychology."
-Seth Klarman

ROI Summary

Return-on-investment can be determined from both an intangible and tangible perspective. To determine the value of the return both should be considered to construct a complete assessment.

Intangible can be related to the human experience and tangible can be related to money – they are *inseparable* in business results.

To follow are 2 great examples of the ROI chain reaction. The first is a chart created at the end of a leadership development initiative. The information is directly from the participants. The "for me" is in reference to what they received from the experience (intangible) and how that was translated to their team (intangible) and then how those translated into measurable, concrete financial benefits to company operations (tangible). It's a good view of the ripple effect and the demonstrated value of leadership development and improving team synergy.

The next are 2 descriptive case studies. Both are examples of tying the human side to the operational-financial side of the business.

Simple ROI Philosophy
You need an intention to measure,
determine what to measure, then
measure it

#1: Final Debriefing Chart | Leadership development initiative to improve cross departmental performance - $250k ROI-6 month impact

INTANGIBLES		TANGIBLES
		#s, %, $
For Me	**For My Team**	**Immediate | Long Term**
Feeling more capable	Trust being built	*Several results reported, here are just a few:*
Confidence		
Better attitude	Better problem solving	$1,500 saved /kept in house – fabrication need due to increased productivity, time available
Feel team is more confident in his leadership	More bonded	
Happy (hated coming to work, was going to step down)	Better rapport and respect	Manufacturing Line – 3 hrs of down time saved in a wk and each week after. appx. $1,500 savings x 6 wks = $9,000 x 6 mths = $54,000
Feels appreciated	Experiencing more efficiency in work	Week 7 – 94% capacity – only 18 minutes of down time. Line start up savings appx./rounded down - $2,400.00 a week (sustained at same level) $2,400 x 24 weeks = $57,600
Better thought process	More confidence	
Gained specific techniques	Better attitudes	
Relief – things are finally getting fixed	Significantly reduced 'shift competition and resentment"	Just these 3 items – total savings for 6 months: $116,700.00
Less stress		
More organized		*Ripple Effect or Impact Map Summary - Intangible to Tangible*
Getting more done	Sense of team work across all shifts = team cohesion	
Getting help		ROI on hourly rate per team member-increased due to substantial uptick in engagement (*meaning* enhanced connection, drive, desire, motivation = applied personal "human resource" to work) raising productivity.
Better communication	Increased morale	
"sees light at the end of the tunnel"	More focused	
excited		
hopeful	Better esteems	Rise in engagement due to implementation of more assertive, intentional leadership coupled with group leadership techniques, which fostered consistent focus, goal achievement, bonding, sense of team, sense of value along with respectful accountability of individual contributions to expectations, continuity between all shifts.
feels good about work and team	Communicating more and better quality	
feel supported		
better prioritizing	More time to be pro-active	
decided to stay and not look for another position	Using, applying in-house talents to special projects vs. farming them out	Increased productivity cleared more time for strategic planning producing proactive activities, which help mitigate machinery down time and available use of little used, but valuable skills for other needs
less fearful of loosing job		
Increased quality of work	Better prioritizing	
Feeling more valued	Greater sense of accomplishment & contribution	

#2: A Case Study | Leadership Development / Department Turnaround

Situation: Inexperienced manager/leader promoted to Director due to strong technical ability; department culture in a highly dysfunctional state from previous leader.

Candidate is a bright, intelligent, likable engineer with great promise, but little experience and training as a leader and manager. Therefore, he is not functioning adequately in this specific area of his responsibilities. He is not very assertive, lacks professional responses, and is not effective in managing his managers and holding them accountable.

Additionally, he has not garnered the level of respect from his team needed to successfully lead. Since he is not fully vested in the leadership role, he is defaulting to "doing the work", and not delegating, which leaves little time for other critical management functions.

Prescribed Action Taken: Initial 3 month 1/1 leadership development coaching engagement, renewed for another 3 months adding leadership/team coaching for all department leaders (superintendents, supervisors, team leads).

Coaching Objectives:
> To build his knowledge in how to effectively manage and lead (will construct a customized training/reference manual from the coaching experience as an ongoing resource post engagement).
> To help him communicate more professionally with all stakeholders
> To create needed leadership and management behaviors (e.g. assertiveness, consistent communication, accountability structure, delegation, time management) that earns the respect of his direct reports and executive leadership within the Tucker facility
> To build his confidence as a competent director/leader
> Get improved outcomes for the entire team
> To continue to increase the morale of the department through his leadership

Results - Return on Investment (all outcomes and more achieved)
ROI in dollars: 10 week net gain $82,360.00
22 week net gain - $164,720.00,
52 week net gain - $454,272.00
ROI in percentage: first 10 weeks: 1,647% // 22 weeks 3,294%

Comment on Results:
President: "I am incredibly pleased the results. It is undeniable the change in his leadership and how his department is functioning. Our down time has been substantially reduced on each lines. I am so surprised that we saw immediate financial impact within the first 2-3 weeks of his coaching."

Results of other training and coaching engagements, all of which have numbers associated with the results.

- ROI on hourly rate per team member-increased due to substantial uptick in engagement (*meaning* enhanced connection, drive, desire, motivation = applied personal "human resource" to work) raising productivity.

- Team members began to care more because they felt cared for -- getting attention and practical help...application of what was being learned with coaching gave them the opportunity to prove to themselves, things could get better. These things can work.

- Rise in engagement due to implementation of more assertive, intentional leadership coupled with group leadership techniques, fostered consistent focus, goal achievement, bonding, sense of team, sense of value along with respectful accountability of individual contributions to expectations, creating continuity between all shifts. This increased confidence and sense of competence.

- A rise in cross-departmental collaboration, increased respect and trust activating a desire to work together, problem solve, be helpful.

- Increased productivity cleared more time for strategic planning producing proactive activities, which help mitigate machinery down time and available use of little used, but valuable skills for other needs.

Closing Thoughts

Simple yet compelling conclusions can be drawn from the content of this briefing and from my experience as an organizational performance/talent management consultant.

The more behavior and financially literate your leadership team becomes; the more profits can be generated.

When you effectively align the people part of your business enterprise (through strategic behavior management) with other resources, processes and strategies you will get meaningful, profitable results.

If you are not getting the results you desire, there is misalignment, similar to when a car is not driving at it's best. Here's what I've discovered, **many leaders have a very high tolerance for misalignment.** They get use to it, ignore, excuse or minimize it and therefore are unwilling to see the cost or pay the cost of repair and that's why literacy is an essential leadership/management competency.

Some companies are driving down the road just fine, but if they received a tune-up would run better, yet they may not recognize they need one. That reminds me of a Jim Collins insight form the book *Good to Great*, "Good is the enemy of great." In either case, whether they invest in help or not, it will cost the company one way or the other.

If you feel as if there might be some "misalignments" within your organization, don't hesitate to connect for a conversation. There are a variety of ways we can help.

How to Use This Briefing
I'll offer some suggestions by way of a few questions:
- ➲ What would be the impact to your organization if every leader and human resource partner knew and understood the content of this briefing.
- ➲ Would it help them be better business partners?

- ➲ Would it improve organizational performance?
- ➲ Could it create the possibility of an improved profit/loss statement?
- ➲ Could It increase the value of your company?

If you answered yes to any of these, here are some recommended action items:

- ➲ Have a leadership roundtable to discuss; determine KPIs (key people indicators)
- ➲ Meet with your human resource department
- ➲ Determine how you want to tie this information to improving operational performance.
- ➲ Determine how to integrate this information in your leadership development plans.

We'd be happy to help. We can facilitate a learning/strategy session to jumpstart your process, uncover areas of misalignment, facilitate an alignment roll-out or address other areas related to improving organizational improvement. No matter what next steps you take, from assimilating the knowledge and insights of this book, you can do so with confidence -- knowing there will be a return-on-investment. Oh what a feeling! That's the power of behavior and financial literacy!

> Anytime you work to create positive, profitable behaviors for one person, you more than likely are going to improve the compensation, return-on-investment for the team members with whom they most closely work *aka*...the ripple effect.

"Most people that derail as leaders in the corporate world, it's not because they couldn't do the math and calculate return on investment properly. The issues are communication and understanding. All of what typically would've been called the 'soft stuff.' You have to be authentic. You have to be dialed into the soft stuff."
Douglas Conant

| More About Us |

▶ RESULTS BASED LEADERSHIP

I've reference through-out this briefing a framework we use to improve operational performance while developing leaders called results-based leadership – marrying both needs. It's an 8-point framework from which leaders execute strategy, process and day-to-day business activity and has proven to have significant, measurable impact and value – providing substantial return-on-investment when implemented.

Additionally, the framework is designed to activate and engage employees contributing to a positive, meaningful employee experience and providing a context to cultivate high performance teams. It's a unique and practical way to improve operations, develop leaders and nurture culture. If you want to increase profits by way of developing managers and leaders, improving employee engagement as well as operational performance, you'll want to learn more or contact us for a preliminary discussion. Go here: https://joanncorley.com/Company-Overview_.html

▶ BONUS MATERIAL

We've set up a web page dedicated to our Executive Briefing series with other relevant material and, as a reminder, access to a free pdf with the purchase of the book. We'll also offer a free pdf version of the book 15 Shifts – the first in our briefing series.
Briefing Page: https://joanncorley.com/Executive_Briefings.html
Contact Info: Em: joann@thehumansphere.com | Phone: 678.826.1721

▶ ABOUT THE AUTHOR

JoAnn Corley is the Founder, CEO of The Human Sphere™, an organizational performance consultancy that helps companies increase earnings through holistic talent management.

She is also a passionate, inspiring business speaker and author. She has shared that passion with thousands through-out North America on such themes as creative & critical thinking, team synergy, results-based leadership, emotional intelligence, and holistic talent management. She has spoken in every major city and state in the U.S.

She is author of several books including 15 Shifts – The Essential Guide to Transform Your Talent Management and Brain On Fire – Unleashing Your Creative Superpowers. She is also the creator of the professional development app – The 1% Edge Portable Coach, available on all smartphone platforms.

Named to several top 100 HR & Management Experts to follow, she has been quoted or featured in articles for NBC News, Huffington Post, Salesforce.com, Monster.com, Harvard Business Review, HR Hero, ATD National, SHRM National, Management Business Daily, Recruiter.com to name a few. She is currently on-going business & leadership contributor to Huffington Post, Recruiter.com and Salesforce.com.

▶ ABOUT OUR COMPANY
The Human Sphere is a boutique organizational performance / talent management consultancy. We partner with companies to help them increase revenue and value by aligning the human side to operations through human-centric, results based leadership, which we call holistic talent management. We work with proven methodologies to ensure immediate and long term results. Even our smallest engagements have generated tremendous value.

▶ USEFUL LINKS
Leadership Blog   www.joanncorleyspeaks.com
Main Website   www.thehumansphere.com
Facebook   www.facebook.com/joanncorley.the1percentcoach
LinkedIn   www.linkedin/in/joanncorley
Google+   https://plus.google.com/+JoAnnCorley
Twitter   @joanncorley

App | The 1% Edge Portable Coach
Amazon Author Page
http://www.amazon.com/JoAnn-R.-Corley/e/B004HGQKZ2

www.ingramcontent.com/pod-product-compliance
Lightning Source LLC
Chambersburg PA
CBHW061443180526
45170CB00004B/1533